Brandon Carpenter

Between Exile and Glory

The Story of the Second Temple and the Faith That Endured

Shalom Falls
Publishing
Wichita Fall, TX

Publisher's Cataloging-in-Publication data Carpenter, Brandon Between Exile and Glory

ISBN 979-8-9995071-9-8 (Paperback)
ISBN 979-8-9956949-0-8 (ePub)
ISBN 979-8-9956949-1-5 (Audio)

Library of Congress Control Number: 2026909662

www.shalomfalls.com

First Published 2026 Shalom Falls

About the Author

Brandon Carpenter is an experienced educator, pastor, and community leader with over 30 years of service in teaching, academic leadership, and faith-based mentorship. Along with completed studies in a Doctor of Ministry in Executive Pastor Leadership from Dallas Theological Seminary, he holds advanced degrees in Christian Apologetics, Biblical Studies, and Education. As founding pastor of *Shalom* Falls Messianic Community in Wichita Falls, Texas, Brandon is dedicated to integrating faith and learning, emphasizing *Yeshua*'s Jewish identity and the authority of the *Torah*.

Learn more about Brandon's ministry at Shalom Falls Messianic Community by visiting www.shalomfalls.com.

To my wife, Dawn—

Thank you for being my constant strength and quiet inspiration. Your patience, encouragement, and faith in me gave this book its heartbeat. Every page carries traces of your love, and I could not have written a single word without the warmth of your presence beside me.

To my son, Thomas—
I love you more than words can ever fully hold. Watching you grow into the person you are has been one of the greatest joys of my life. Your brilliance amazes me—I'll admit, I'm a little envious of it—and your character makes me endlessly proud. This work, in some small way, is for you and because of you.

To my daughter, Hannah—
Your love amazes me more than I can ever fully express. The way you care, the way you give, and the way you stand strong in who you are is something I deeply admire. Your strength is steady and beautiful, and it has taught me more than you may ever realize. I am so proud of you and grateful every day to be your father.

Table of Contents

Preface   1

Part I: Exile and New Beginnings   9

   1 When the Fire Fell   10

   2 Return and Rebuilding   23

   3 A People of the Book   36

   4 When Greece Came East   50

Part II: Foreign Kings and Faithful Hearts   60

   5 War for the Holy Place   61

   6 Kings and Priests   74

Part III: Rome, Revival, and Revelation   87

   7 Herod's Kingdom   88

   8 Many Voices, One Hope   101

   9 Scrolls by the Dead Sea   118

   10 Messiah and the Temple   132

Part IV: Destruction and New Life   143

   11 The Last Stand   144

   12 Faith Without a Temple   154

Part V: The Temple that Lives On   164

   13 From Ruins to Renewal   165

   14 Early Disciples   173

   15 A Vision of Restoration   184

Epilogue The Enduring House of God   194

Discussion Questions   198

Bibliography   218

Appendices   223

Preface

The story of the Second Temple period is not merely a chapter of ancient history. It is the story of faith rediscovered after disaster, of worship renewed in the shadow of empire, and of hope kindled amid uncertainty. From the smoldering ruins of Solomon's Temple in 586 BCE to the destruction of Herod's Temple in 70 CE, the Jewish people lived through five centuries of extraordinary transformation. Those centuries shaped not only Judaism as it exists today but also the world into which *Yeshua* of Nazareth was born and through which the first followers of His teachings would move.

To understand the Scriptures, whether *Torah*, Prophets, or Gospels, one must understand this period. The ideas, debates, and expectations that defined Jewish life in the Second Temple era still echo every time we open the Bible, sing a psalm, or pray for redemption.

Why the Second Temple Period Still Matters

Imagine what it means to lose the center of your worship, your national symbol, and your sense of divine nearness all at once. That was the reality facing the people of Judah when Babylon leveled Jerusalem and carried its people into exile. The ancient Israelites lived with a deep conviction that God's presence dwelt among them in the Temple. It was a house not only of stone, but of divine promise. When that house fell, their worldview collapsed with it. How could they worship the God of Israel in a foreign land? Had His covenant failed?

Yet out of that trauma, something unexpected was born. The Second Temple period began as an era of rebuilding, but it became an era of redefinition. Deprived of the old structures, Israel learned to find God in new places. They discovered His presence in the scroll, in the synagogue, and in the rhythm of prayer. The synagogue, the *Torah* reading cycle, the daily liturgy are all hallmarks of Jewish life today. All grew from the soil of exile and restoration.

This is why the Second Temple period matters. It is the story of survival that became transformation. It shows how faith can outlive catastrophe, how God's people can remain His people even without land, king, or temple. Every generation since has drawn strength from that truth.

But there is more. For followers of *Yeshua*, the Second Temple era is the stage upon which His life and message unfold. The Gospel writers assumed their readers understood a world filled with priests, festivals, purity laws, and competing sects. All were products of the late Second Temple period. The debates between Pharisees and Sadducees, the longing for a Messiah who would purify the Temple, the deep sense that Israel's story remained unfinished. These were not background details. Rather, they were the heartbeat of the age.

When we grasp what the Second Temple meant to the people of its time, *Yeshua*'s words come alive with fresh clarity. His parables about vineyards, tenants, and the Kingdom of Heaven speak directly to Jewish hopes and fears born in the shadow of empire. His lament over Jerusalem, "How often I longed to gather your children together," is no longer a poetic phrase but a cry rooted in centuries of longing for divine restoration.

The Second Temple period also offers modern readers a lens for understanding continuity between Jewish and Christian faiths. It reminds us that the New Testament was not the beginning of God's story but a continuation of it. The first believers did not invent a new religion from whole cloth. Instead, they were part of an ongoing dialogue about covenant, purity, and redemption. These questions already orbiting Jewish hearts in the time of Ezra and the prophets, the Maccabees and the Pharisees, and the Zealots and the Essenes.

To read the history of the Second Temple period is, therefore, to enter the shared story of Israel and the Church. This is a story of faith tested in exile, renewed through worship, and transformed through hope in the coming presence of God.

How to Read This Book

This book is written to bring that story to life not only for historians or theologians, but for readers who love Scripture and desire to understand it more deeply. It moves chronologically from the fall of the First Temple through the rebuilding under Persian rule, the struggles of the Hellenistic age, the rise of Rome, and finally, the destruction of the Second Temple in 70 CE. Each chapter invites you to see the people of Israel not as distant figures but as fellow believers wrestling with timeless questions. How do we live when God seems far away? What does it mean to be faithful under foreign power? Where is hope to be found when the sacred is lost?

You will not need any prior background in ancient history to follow this journey. The goal is clarity, not complexity. Historical events are woven into narrative and reflection, combining archaeological insight with biblical imagery to create a living picture of the times. The body of the text remains a story of faith, perseverance, and transformation.

To gain the most from this book, you might read it in one of three ways:

1. As a historical journey. Move through the chapters as you would a story, following the thread of Israel's return, revival, and resilience.

2. As a devotional companion. Pause after each chapter to reflect on how themes of exile and renewal mirror your own journey of faith. Many readers find, within these ancient struggles, a mirror to modern spiritual life.

3. As a tool for communal study. Small groups, classes, and congregations can easily adapt the material for group reading. Discussion questions or study prompts (available at the end of the book) connect the narrative to Scripture and practical faith.

Each section concludes with a brief reflection linking the era's history to its spiritual lessons. The rise of the synagogue may invite us to think about how community sustains worship in times of loss. The Maccabean revolt may challenge us to consider what we are willing to defend in our faith. The destruction of the temple may lead us to ponder where God dwells when all visible signs of His presence are gone.

Throughout, the aim is balance. A call to remain faithful to history while attentive to theology, and to honor both Jewish and Christian perspectives without diminishing either. The story of the Second Temple belongs to both communities, and indeed to all who trace their faith to Abraham's God.

Reading this book is therefore an act of rediscovery. It helps us see that between exile and glory lies a long middle ground. A place where God shapes His people not in triumph, but in endurance. God renews His nation not through kings and armies, but through prophets, teachers, and common worshipers who refused to forget His name.

A Timeline of Key Events

To set the stage, here is a simple timeline of major moments in the Second Temple era. These events will unfold in detail throughout the chapters that follow:

586 BCE – Babylon conquers Jerusalem, destroys the First Temple, and carries many Israelites into exile.

539 BCE – Cyrus the Great of Persia captures Babylon and issues an edict allowing exiled peoples, including the Jews, to return home.

516 BCE – The Second Temple is completed in Jerusalem under Zerubbabel's leadership, and Temple worship resumes.

458 BCE – Ezra the scribe arrives in Jerusalem, initiating religious reform centered on *Torah* reading and obedience.

445 BCE – Nehemiah rebuilds the walls of Jerusalem, reestablishing the city's identity.

332 BCE – Alexander the Great conquers the Persian Empire, introducing Hellenistic culture to the Near East.

167–164 BCE – The Maccabean Revolt erupts after Antiochus IV Epiphanes desecrates the Temple. The

Hasmonean family reclaims and rededicates it. This is the event commemorated in Hanukkah.

142–63 BCE – The Hasmonean dynasty rules an independent Jewish kingdom, expanding territory and centralizing priestly power.

63 BCE – Roman general Pompey enters Jerusalem, and Judea becomes a client state of Rome.

37–4 BCE – Herod the Great rules Judea under Roman authority. He renovates and expands the Second Temple, making it one of the grandest structures of the ancient world.

4 BCE–30 CE – The life and ministry of *Yeshua* of Nazareth take place in a Judea governed by Roman procurators and alive with Messianic expectation.

66–70 CE – The Jewish revolt against Rome leads to the destruction of Jerusalem and the Second Temple by Titus's army.

This sequence of events represents not only political changes but spiritual turning points. With each new era, Persian, Greek, and Roman, the Jewish people faced fresh challenges to their identity. Yet through each test, they adapted while preserving their core conviction that the covenant between God and Israel would endure forever.

The Heart of the Foreword

In reading about the Second Temple, we are not gazing into a museum case. We are entering the living memory of faith. The prophets and scribes, priests and peasants who fill these pages are bound to us by a shared struggle. The struggle to believe when the evidence seems against belief, and to hope when history appears to have closed its doors.

For Jewish readers, this book invites a fresh encounter with the resilience that birthed Judaism as a religion of prayer, study, and ethical life. For Christian readers, it offers insight into the spiritual soil from which *Yeshua*'s teachings grew. It was a world of festivals, psalms, and promises in which the Kingdom of God was not a new idea, but the long-awaited fulfillment of Israel's story. For all readers, Jewish or Christian, it is a reminder that faith is never static. Rather, it is always being reformed in response to exile and revelation, loss and renewal.

In many ways, we still live in the aftermath of 70 CE. The temple stones remain scattered, but the hope of rebuilding has never faded. Every prayer, every gathering, and every act of mercy continues the legacy of those who kept their faith alive in the Second Temple years.

May this book rekindle that same endurance in us. May it remind us that even when the walls fall, God's presence is never gone. Although empires rise and fall, God's covenant endures. The journey from exile to glory is not only Israel's story, but ours as well.

How This Book Came to Be

As with most of my books, the content of this book originated from a fourteen-week adult Bible study I taught at a church I pastored in Wichita Falls, Texas. The manuscripts of each lesson were saved on my hard drive for over 15 years. After receiving many encouraging messages to compile these Bible studies into a book, I am motivated to bring together these manuscripted lessons into the contents of the book you are now reading. Like many evangelicals, I was unaware of the formation of

Judaism and the impact of the Second Temple Period on the people of Israel before conducting my research on this topic fifteen years ago. I often wondered why Pharisees, Sadducees, and places like synagogues were mentioned in the opening pages of the New Testament but were absent in the Hebrew Scriptures. This book aims to provide answers to these questions.

Throughout each chapter, there are numerous footnotes. In addition to providing bibliographic information, these footnotes were derived from answered questions or "rabbit trails" that were explored during each lesson. Many footnotes provide additional information to an idea, attitude, deed, or tradition introduced in a paragraph.

Part I: Exile and New Beginnings

1
When the Fire Fell
The Destruction of Solomon's Temple

Smoke rose over Jerusalem like a dark pillar against the summer sky. The sound of Babylonian battering rams, the clash of swords, and the weeping of priests filled the valley. It was the ninth of *Av*, 586 BCE when the fire fell upon the House of *Adonai*.

For four centuries the Temple had stood as the heartbeat of Israel's worship. Every morning the *kohanim* trimmed the lamps and offered incense. During every festival, pilgrims ascended singing the Psalms of Ascent. The Temple was more than grand architecture. It was the meeting place between heaven and earth, the tangible sign that the covenant God of Israel dwelled among His people.

Now, after a long siege, famine, and the betrayal of hope, the unthinkable happened. Nebuchadnezzar's forces broke through the wall. The Babylonians stripped the gold from the doors, plundered the sacred vessels, and set fire to the House of God (2 Kings 25:8-9).[1] The air filled with

---

[1] In the ancient Near Eastern worldview, temples were the earthly houses of the gods, and their cult vessels were tangible signs of a deity's presence, wealth, and power. When Nebuchadnezzar plundered vessels from the Jerusalem Temple and placed them "in the house of his god" in Babylon, this publicly proclaimed that Babylon's gods had defeated Israel's God and now owned His treasures. Victorious kings routinely displayed captured temple objects in their own sanctuaries as war trophies, dramatizing the supposed triumph of their deities over the gods of conquered

the smell of cedar, olive oil, and burning flesh. Once the people of Israel sung, "Blessed is the man who comes in the name of *Adonai!*" (Psalm 118:26) Now, they cried out from the streets, "By the rivers of Babylon, there we sat down and wept, when we remembered Zion. On the willows there we hung up our harps . . . How can we sing *Adonai*'s song in a foreign land?" (Psalm 137:1-2, 4)

The people who had believed that *Adonai*'s presence dwelled in that holy house suddenly faced an unbearable question, Had God abandoned His dwelling place?

In truth, the fire that consumed the Temple revealed more than military might. It exposed the spiritual sickness of a nation that had ignored countless warnings. Jeremiah had spoken it clearly, "Because you have forsaken Me and burned incense to other gods . . . therefore I will cast you out of this land into a land that you do not know." (Jeremiah 16:11-13)

When the fire fell, covenant unfaithfulness met divine justice. But even then, the story was not over. The ashes of Jerusalem would become the soil for the renewal of faith.

The Trauma of Exile

The siege of Jerusalem produced starvation beyond imagination. Mothers boiled grain husks and children cried for bread in empty streets. When the Babylonians entered the city, they slaughtered resisters and deported thousands of survivors to Babylon. Those left behind were

---

peoples. Daniel 1:2 explicitly notes that the Temple vessels were carried to the treasure house of Nebuchadnezzar's god, emphasizing that, in Babylonian ideology, Judah's defeat validated the superiority of Marduk and the Babylonian pantheon.

the very poor, tasked with tending the vineyards and fields (2 Kings 25:12). Nebuchadnezzar ordered the execution of priests and royal advisors, dismantled the palace, and carried off the sacred furnishings. What had once been filled with music and sacrifice now stood silent, a mountain of ash on Mount Zion.

For the exiles, Babylon was both alien and alluring. The empire was vast, wealthy, and religiously pluralistic. Its kingdom was filled with temples to Marduk, Ishtar, and other deities. The Israelites who found themselves there were strangers in every sense. Linguistically, culturally, and spiritually, they are completely out of their element. They hung their harps on the trees, symbols of worship now unused because their hearts were broken.

The trauma of exile cannot be overstated. Their identity, land, Temple, priesthood, and monarchy, were all stripped away. The covenant promises given to *Avraham*, *Yitz'chak*, and *Ya'akov* seemed suspended in midair.

Some clung to despair, whispering that the God of Israel had been defeated by the gods of Babylon.[2] Others began to ask harder questions. Could *Adonai* still be

---

[2] Ancient Near Eastern peoples generally saw warfare as a contest between deities, not merely armies, so a defeated nation signaled that its god had been outmatched or had withdrawn favor. Royal inscriptions often portray kings marching to war "at the command" of their god, who goes with them as a divine warrior and grants victory, making military success a public validation of that deity's power. Conversely, when a city fell, people interpreted it as judgment from their own god or triumph by the enemy's god; practices like "godnapping," seizing a conquered people's divine statues, symbolized that their deity had lost control. Biblical and surrounding texts share this worldview but also subvert it by insisting that Israel's God can use foreign armies as instruments of judgment, so Israel's defeat does not mean *Adonai*'s defeat, but His disciplinary action.

worshiped in a land not His own? Could holiness survive without sacrifice?[3]

Over time, small groups began meeting in homes along the riverbanks.[4] They recited from memory the words of the *Torah*. Fathers taught sons the stories of creation, exodus, and covenant. Mothers whispered the Psalms at night. What had begun in tears slowly hardened into determination. If the Temple could not stand, the people themselves would become its living walls. "For thus says *Adonai*: 'When seventy years for Babylon are complete, I will remember you and confirm My good word toward you, to bring you back to this place. For I know the plans

---

[3] Ancient Israelites asked questions like "Can *Adonai* be worshiped in a foreign land?" because exile shattered their inherited ancient Near Eastern worldview about regional gods and sacred space. In surrounding cultures, each deity was linked to a specific land and people; divine authority was normally territorial, so crossing a border meant entering the domain of another god. Early Israelite religion largely shared this assumption: YHWH was seen as Israel's national deity, specially associated with the land promised to Abraham and with Zion as His dwelling. When Jerusalem fell and the people were deported, many assumed that removal from the land meant distance from YHWH Himself, prompting laments like, "How can we sing the Lord's song in a foreign land?" in Psalm 137. Prophets such as Ezekiel answered by revealing that *Adonai* could be "a sanctuary" for His people even in exile, gradually transforming this older regional conception.

[4] Ancient Israelites (and later Jews) often met and prayed along riverbanks in exile and diaspora because flowing water provided both ritual and practical needs. Rivers supplied "living water" for required washings and ablutions before prayer and study, especially where no *mikveh* or built synagogue existed. In foreign cities, minority religious gatherings were sometimes pushed outside the walls, so a quiet riverside became a natural, tolerated meeting place. Psalm 137 pictures exiles sitting and weeping "by the rivers of Babylon," where they remembered Zion and struggled with how to sing *Adonai*'s songs in a foreign land, suggesting the riverside became a locus of communal grief, memory, and worship. This pattern continues into the Second Temple and New Testament era, where Jews in places like Philippi met by a river "where prayer was customary."

that I have in mind for you,' declares *Adonai*, 'plans for *shalom* and not calamity—to give you a future and a hope.'" (Jeremiah 29:10-11)

That promise became their heartbeat. Even while captives, they carried in their hearts the certainty that the covenant had not died in the fire.

Prophets in a Foreign Land

Exile is often thought of as silence. However, within that silence, the voice of God thundered anew through prophets who re-imagined faith for a displaced people.

Jeremiah: The Weeping Watchman

Jeremiah had witnessed Jerusalem's fall and chose to remain with the remnant. His tears recorded in Scripture are not mere emotion. Rather, they are theology in its rawest form. His scroll, *Eichah* (Lamentations) reads like an eyewitness account of devastation. "How lonely sits the city once great with people! She who was great among the nations has become like a widow." (Lamentations 1:1) Yet amid the ruins he discovered the pulse of divine mercy. "The mercies of *Adonai* are new every morning; great is Your faithfulness." (Lamentations 3:23)

Jeremiah sent letters to the exiles instructing them to build houses, plant gardens, and seek the welfare of Babylon, for "in its *shalom* you will have *shalom*" (Jeremiah 29:7). That counsel defied expectation. Rather than urging rebellion, he taught patient faith. Babylon would not have the final word. Only *Adonai* has that right.

Ezekiel: Glory on the Wheels

Among those exiled early, before Jerusalem fell, was the priest Ezekiel. Settled with the community at *Tel Abib* by the Chebar Canal, Ezekiel experienced visions unveiling that *Adonai*'s presence was not confined to the destroyed sanctuary.

He saw the glory of the Lord (*kavod Adonai*) depart from Jerusalem, borne aloft by living creatures and wheels within wheels (Ezekiel 10). This vision would have shattered any remaining assumption that God's presence was static. He was, and remains, the mobile, sovereign, and uncontained.

Later, Ezekiel saw something more astounding. His vision asserting the same glory returning to a future, restored Temple (Ezekiel 43:4-5). By that vision, the exiles learned that the covenant God had not left them. The God of their covenant traveled with them and promised eventual renewal.[5]

Ezekiel also unveiled the principle that personal repentance matters. "The soul who sins will die," he

---

[5] Several key biblical and rabbinic texts state that when Israel is in exile, their God is with them. Ezekiel 11:16 affirms that God tells the exiles that although He has scattered them among the nations, He will be "a sanctuary" for them in the lands where they have gone, affirming His presence with them outside the Land. Isaiah 63:9 states, "In all their afflictions, He was afflicted" and is read as teaching that God shares the suffering of Israel even in their troubles and dispersions. Rabbinic literature also teaches that God is with His people in exile. *Talmud Bavli, Megillah* 29a, "Every place to which they were exiled, the *Shechinah* went with them . . . When they went to Egypt, the *Shechinah* was with them . . . to Babylonia . . . to Edom . . . and when they are redeemed, the Shechinah will return with them." *Midrashic* traditions "God in Exile (*Shechinah b'Galuta*)" explicitly state that whenever Israel is exiled, the *Shechinah* is exiled with them and will return with them at the redemption.

declared, "but if the wicked turns from his sin . . . he will surely live." (Ezekiel 18:20-21) The covenant was not a group membership card. Rather, it was a living relationship renewed by each heart.

Daniel: Faith under Empire

While Ezekiel ministered among the exiles, Daniel served in the Babylonian court itself. From his youth, Daniel resolved not to defile himself, even amid royal luxury (Daniel 1:8). [6] When commanded to bow before idols, he refused. When forbidden to pray, he opened his window toward Jerusalem and prayed three times a day.[7]

His faith transformed captivity into testimony. Through dreams and visions, Daniel revealed that all kingdoms belong to the Most High. Babylon, Persia, Greece, and Rome would all rise and fall, but "the God of

---

[6] Daniel resolved not to be defiled by the king's rich food and wine, which likely included non-kosher animals and meat and drink offered to idols. He respectfully requested an alternative, proposing a ten-day test in which he and his friends would eat only vegetables (*zeroim*, "seeds") and drink water, foods that avoided idolatrous contamination and suspect meat. At the end of the trial they appeared healthier than the others, so the official allowed them to continue this disciplined, quasi-kosher diet within the Babylonian court.

[7] Traditional Jewish practice centers on three daily prayer services: *Shacharit, Mincha,* and *Ma'ariv. Shacharit* is the morning service, typically the longest, including blessings, Psalms, *Shema,* and *Amidah,* orienting the day around gratitude and dependence on God. *Mincha,* the afternoon service, is brief but spiritually strategic, interrupting the workday with *Ashrei* and the *Amidah* to re-focus the heart and priorities toward God. *Ma'ariv (Arvit),* the evening service, expresses trust in God's protection through the night and includes Shema with its blessings and the *Amidah.* Rabbinic tradition roots these three times either in the patriarchs—*Avraham, Yitzchak,* and *Ya'akov*—or in the daily Temple sacrifices, and halachah fixes them as the basic framework of Jewish daily prayer

heaven will set up a kingdom that will never be destroyed." (Daniel 2:44)

Daniel's unwavering devotion showed that integrity in exile can reveal the power of God to rulers and nations. His story echoes through every generation that faces persecution or diaspora. He demonstrated that the faithful heart can thrive even in the court of its oppressors.

Learning to Seek God Without a Temple

When the fire fell on the stones of Jerusalem, it ignited a flame of discovery within the human spirit. With the altar gone, how could Israel approach their God? Their answer changed history. In place of sacrifice came Scripture. Scrolls that survived the devastation became more precious than gold. The exiles gathered to read the words of Moses aloud, and the *Torah* became the new sanctuary. Where once blood had sealed atonement, now hearing and obeying became the sacrifice of the heart. "To obey is better than sacrifice." (1 Samuel 15:22)

From those gatherings would emerge the institution later known as the synagogue. The synagogue became a meeting place for prayer, study, and community.[8] What had been born of loss became a means of perseverance that would sustain Jewish life for millennia. The Word became

---

[8] The destruction of the Temple and earlier exilic experiences led to an increased emphasis on Torah study, prayer, and communal gatherings that eventually developed into the synagogue institution (Nehemiah 8:1–8; cf. Hosea 6:6; 1 Samuel 15:22). See Shaye J. D. Cohen, *From the Maccabees to the Mishnah* (Louisville: Westminster John Knox, 2014), 134–156; Lee I. Levine, *The Ancient Synagogue: The First Thousand Years* (New Haven: Yale University Press, 2005); and E. P. Sanders, *Judaism: Practice and Belief 63 BCE–66 CE* (Philadelphia: Trinity Press, 1992).

portable holiness. Whether by a riverbank or in a foreign city square, a scroll could open heaven.

Exile birthed a renewed emphasis on *teshuvah*, which means "return" or "repentance."[9] Without the Temple's rituals, atonement became an inner issue of the heart. The words of Psalm 51 took on fresh urgency, "The sacrifices of God are a broken spirit. A broken and a contrite heart, O God, You will not despise." (Psalm 51:19)

Repentance offered restoration wherever one stood. To turn back to *Adonai* became itself a form of worship. The community learned that holiness was not confined to Levites or altars but available to every heart willing to humble itself before the Holy One.

This inward turn marked a profound theological transition. Israel discovered that sin and forgiveness could be addressed through contrition and obedience rather than ritual alone. It was the seed of a spirituality that would blossom in later generations. An issue that both *Yeshua* and the early believers would affirm and expand.

The Sabbath as Sanctuary in Time

Deprived of a Temple's sacred space, the exiles sanctified time. The Sabbath became their temple in

---

[9] Second Temple Jews saw *teshuvah* as God's appointed way to restore covenant relationship, both for individuals and for all Israel. Texts like Ben Sira emphasize that God grants "a return" to those who repent and praises His great mercy toward all who turn back to Him. Later, other Second Temple writings, such as Jubilees and Qumran literature, frame national restoration and end-time forgiveness in terms of Israel's repentance, sometimes even viewing repentance itself as divinely enabled. In this period, *teshuvah* is not only regret but a decisive turning from sin to wholehearted obedience, opening the way for forgiveness, renewed blessing, and eschatological hope.

rhythm and a sanctified day unshaken by empire. Each week, they remembered creation and covenant, "As for you, speak to the children of Israel, saying, 'Surely you must keep My *Shabbatot* . . . It is a sign between Me and you throughout your generations'" (Exodus 31:13).

Lighting Sabbath lamps in Babylon was an act of holy defiance.[10] It was a declaration that even here, far from Zion, *Adonai* ruled over time itself. Every seventh day was a rehearsal for redemption.

A God Too Great for One House

Above all, exile shattered the ancient assumption that God's physical dwelling was limited to a geographical site. Ezekiel's vision had already shown the *kavod* of *Adonai* moving freely across the world. Solomon had once prayed at the Temple's dedication, "But will God really dwell on the earth? Behold, heaven and the highest heaven cannot contain You!" (1 Kings 8:27)

The exile transformed that theological statement into existential truth. *Adonai* was not the local deity of a small hill country. Rather, He was the universal King. The gods

---

[10] For Judeans in Babylon, lighting Sabbath lamps became a quiet but potent act of holy resistance. The Temple lay in ruins, sacrifices had ceased, and imperial power pressed them to forget Zion and blend into Babylonian life, yet *Shabbat* remained a covenant sign and identity marker they could still keep in their homes. Kindling lamps at sundown publicly marked sacred time, proclaiming that *Adonai*—not Marduk—ordered their week, their labor, and their rest. In early Second Temple consciousness, Sabbath observance was understood as a key cause of the exile when neglected and a key path to renewal when honored; therefore, faithfully welcoming *Shabbat* in a foreign land affirmed hope that God would restore them and "the Sabbath would keep Israel" even in diaspora.

of Babylon were bound to idols of wood and stone, but Israel's God walked the heavens and the waters.

This understanding forever changed the character of Israel's faith. When they finally returned and rebuilt the Temple, they did so knowing that God's presence is never limited to walls. The exile taught them what even Solomon's wisdom could not fully convey. The Almighty desires a dwelling not only on Mount Zion but also in the humble and contrite heart (Isaiah 57:15).

The Slow Birth of Renewal

Out of judgment came the promise of renewal. The prophet Isaiah wrote to exiles yet unborn and spoke words that must have sounded like music. "Comfort, comfort My people, says your God. Speak kindly to Jerusalem . . . that her warfare has been completed, that her iniquity has been pardoned." (Isaiah 40:1-2)

He proclaimed that a highway would be prepared in the wilderness and that every valley would be lifted. Hope began to bloom again beside the rivers of Babylon. When the Persians later conquered Babylon, that hope turned to action. Cyrus' decree (Ezra 1) opened the way for return. The seventy years Jeremiah had foretold were fulfilled, making a return to Zion possible.

Yet the spiritual restoration was already underway long before the first stones were laid for the Second Temple. Exile taught the people to reinterpret the meaning of being the covenant community, emphasizing the idea of carrying holiness within themselves rather than surrounding them.

Lessons for Every Generation

The destruction of Solomon's Temple stands as both tragedy and teacher. It illustrates what happens when faith becomes complacent. Yet it also reveals how divine mercy can rebuild what human failure destroys. Each of its lessons speaks powerfully today.

1. Faith must not depend on circumstance. The exiles learned that presence, not place, sustains relationship with God. Our own faith, too, must survive when sanctuaries close or certainty collapses.

2. Repentance restores the covenant faster than rebuilding. A contrite heart can rise from ashes before bricks ever meet mortar.

3. Scripture is portable holiness. Every time we open the Word, we stand on sacred ground, just as the exiles did by the Chebar Canal.

4. Hope is an act of resistance. To sing in exile is one of the greatest demonstrations of spiritual courage. Each psalm voiced in Babylon defied despair and declared, "*Adonai* still reigns."

A Foreshadowing of Things to Come

Centuries later, *Yeshua* of Nazareth walked the same Temple mount rebuilt by Herod, and He wept as He looked over Jerusalem. His words echoed the same prophetic warning Jeremiah had once spoken, "Not one stone will be left upon another." (Luke 19:44) Yet His promise also fulfilled Ezekiel's message that God would grant His Spirit to dwell within human hearts.

When the Second Temple would fall in 70 CE, faith would once again survive not because of stones, but because of the Spirit. The lessons learned in Babylon would ensure that Judaism and the Messianic hope would not perish with the structure. The fire could not consume faith forged in exile.

Reflection: When Our Own Temples Fall

Every believer eventually faces a period of exile, a time when the fundamental structures of life, health, ministry, community, and confidence collapse. We ask the same ancient questions, where is God now? Has He departed because my world has burned down?

The story of Jerusalem's destruction whispers the answer that the same God who allowed the fire also walks with His people through the smoke. His presence is mobile, merciful, and creative. When our personal temples crumble, remember:

- Babylon's rivers. Even there, the Spirit sings.
- Jeremiah's tears. Grief and faith can share the same breath.
- Ezekiel's wheels. Glory can move.
- Daniel's prayer. Integrity shines brightest in foreign courts.

Through their endurance, we learn to find God not merely in triumph but in transformation. Exile proved that the Holy One of Israel is Emmanuel. God is with us even in judgment, even in distance, even in the dark. The fire that once consumed cedar and gold forged a faith that cannot be burned.

2
Return and Rebuilding:
Hope Restored in Jerusalem

Seventy years had come and gone since the fire consumed Solomon's Temple. Babylon's empire that was once unimaginable in power had crumbled like dust before a new force rising from the east. The Persians under King Cyrus played upon history's stage as instruments of *Adonai*'s mercy.

What human hands called politics and conquest, Scripture called providence. Isaiah had foreseen it more than a century before Cyrus's birth, "Thus says *Adonai* to His anointed, to Cyrus, whose right hand I have grasped, to subdue nations before him . . . It is for the sake of Jacob My servant, and Israel My chosen one . . . so that they may know from the rising of the sun to its setting, that there is none beside Me." (Isaiah 45:1-6)

When the decree finally came, it sounded like the end of exile and the beginning of hope. The scroll read, "Thus says King Cyrus of Persia: *Adonai*, the God of heaven, has given me all the kingdoms of the earth. He has commanded me to build Him a house in Jerusalem . . . Whoever among you belongs to His people, may his God be with him! Let him go up." (Ezra 1:2–3) No trumpet announced this day, yet heaven must have thundered with joy. The exile that began with fire now met freedom through favor.

The Return: Dust, Ruins, and Determination

The journey home was both thrilling and heartbreaking. Those who set out were descendants of the exiles, raised in Babylonian cities, speaking a mix of Aramaic and Hebrew. But they carried with them a burning desire to see Zion again.

Led by the prince Zerubbabel, heir of David's line, and the high priest *Yehoshua* (Joshua) son of *Yehotzadak*, nearly fifty thousand exiles began the long trek of roughly 900 miles westward through the Fertile Crescent. Ezra records that Persian officials returned the sacred vessels Nebuchadnezzar had seized decades earlier. Treasures of gold and silver once used in Solomon's Temple were restored to the Land (Ezra 1:7-11).

When the caravan finally reached Jerusalem, silence greeted them. The walls were piles of rubble, the Temple mount overgrown with weeds. Jackals roamed where pilgrims once sang psalms. Yet their grief quickly gave way to resolve, as the people pitched their tents among the ruins and lifted their eyes toward heaven. They knew what must be done: rebuild the House of God.

Before any stone was set, before any wall was patched, they built an altar. "Then *Yehoshua* son of *Yehotzadak* and his fellow *kohanim* arose, along with Zerubbabel son of Shealtiel . . . and built the altar of the God of Israel to offer burnt offerings on it, as it is written in the *Torah* of Moses." (Ezra 3:2)

Standing amid debris, fire and sacrifice once again rose to heaven. The act was small in scale yet demonstrated a decisive meaning. The exiles declared that worship came first. Consecration precedes construction, and heart before architecture.

They celebrated *Sukkot*, the Feast of Booths, even though no permanent booths surrounded them.[11] Their willingness to worship before the walls or Temple were restored testified to faith learned in Babylon. *Adonai*'s presence is not limited to polished gold. Rather, He dwells where hearts are humbled.

Restoration, however, never comes without resistance. The neighboring peoples who were descendants of the Assyrian policy of forced resettlement offered to help build, claiming to worship the same God. However, the leaders discerned mixed motives and declined. "You have nothing to do with us in building a house for our God." (Ezra 4:3)

Offended, those neighbors under Persian administration began to threaten and lobby against the Judeans. Letters of accusation reached distant capitals, and work on the Temple halted for nearly two decades. For many, discouragement set in. Fields needed tending, houses needed roofs, and survival required compromise. Why pour effort into sacred work that might draw hostility? The prophet Haggai answered that question with

---

[11] *Sukkot*, the Festival of Booths or Tabernacles, is a joyful, weeklong Jewish holiday beginning on the 15th of *Tishrei*, five days after *Yom Kippur*. It combines thanksgiving for the autumn harvest with remembrance of Israel's 40 years of wandering in the wilderness, dwelling in fragile shelters under God's protection. Central to the festival is the *sukkah*, a temporary hut with a leafy roof through which the sky is visible, where families eat, host guests, and sometimes sleep, making the *sukkah* their primary dwelling for seven days. Another key practice is taking the Four Species—*lulav* (palm), *etrog* (citron), *hadassim* (myrtle), and *aravot* (willow)—and waving them in six directions to acknowledge God's presence everywhere and to pray for life-giving rain in the coming year. Sukkot is thus marked by joy, hospitality, and gratitude.

uncompromising clarity, "This people say: 'The time has not come, the time for *Adonai*'s House to be rebuilt.' Then the word of *Adonai* came through Haggai the prophet, saying, 'Is it a time for you yourselves to dwell in your paneled houses, while this House lies in ruins?'" (Haggai 1:2–4)

The prophet confronted complacency with heavenly economics, asserting that until the people prioritized worship, no harvest would suffice. Haggai's words struck deep. The remnant obeyed, stirred by a divine awakening. Zerubbabel resumed leadership, Yehoshua lifted the priests' hands, and work began anew. The labor was not with imperial strength, but with divine spirit. "'Not by might, nor by power, but by My *Ruach*,' says *Adonai-Tzva'ot*." (Zechariah 4:6)

The Second Temple Completed

In the sixth year of King Darius I (516 BCE), the new House of God was finished. Though far smaller than Solomon's, its completion marked covenant renewal. When the builders laid the foundation years earlier and remembering former glory, older priests had wept while the younger shouted with joy (Ezra 3:12-13). At last, those tears now mingled into thanksgiving.

The people kept the Feast of Passover with one heart.[12] "The children of Israel who had returned from the exile

---

[12] Passover, or *Pesach*, is a major spring festival that commemorates God's deliverance of the Israelites from slavery in Egypt and the "passing over" of the marked Israelite homes during the tenth plague. Beginning on the 15th of Nisan, it lasts seven days in Israel and eight days in most communities outside Israel. The feast day centers on the seder, a structured ritual meal that retells the Exodus

kept the Passover on the fourteenth day of the first month . . . They ate it together with all who had separated themselves from the uncleanness of the peoples of the land." (Ezra 6:19, 21)

Thus, the exiles became a worshiping community renewed by grace. Their journey from despair to dedication mirrors the spiritual cycle of repentance leading to rebuilding and rebuilding leading to redeemed joy that every believer has discovered.

Ezra: The Scribe of Renewal

Half a century after the Temple's completion, a new spiritual challenge emerged. The community was rebuilt outwardly yet inwardly drift again threatened holiness. Into that moment walked Ezra the scribe, a descendant of Aaron and scholar of *Torah*. "He was a scribe skilled in the *Torah* of Moses . . . for Ezra had set his heart to seek the *Torah* of *Adonai*, to observe and to teach its statutes and ordinances in Israel." (Ezra 7:6, 10)

Ezra arrived in Jerusalem with royal sanction and a mission to restore covenant fidelity. He carried the authority of the king, but his true power came from passionate faith and exhaustive knowledge of Scripture. When he read the *Torah* publicly and explained its meaning, hearts were pierced. People realized that

---

story through readings from the *Haggadah*, questions, and symbolic foods. Leaven (*chametz*) is removed from homes, and Jews eat unleavened bread, *matzah*, recalling the haste of departure from Egypt. The seder plate typically includes bitter herbs, salt water, a roasted shank bone, egg, greens, and a sweet paste (*haroset*), each representing aspects of slavery and redemption. Passover emphasizes freedom, faithfulness, and transmitting this foundational story to future generations.

survival alone was not enough, and that obedience must define life anew. The exiles' descendants repented, reforming marriages, renewing tithes, rebuilding communal trust.

Ezra's reformation recentered Israel upon Word and worship. The synagogue tradition expanded. Scribes multiplied copies of Scripture, and the public reading of *Torah* became the heartbeat of Jewish communal life. This remains an enduring legacy still witnessed in every congregation today.

Nehemiah: Rebuilding the Walls

While Ezra re-established inner devotion, Nehemiah, cupbearer to King Artaxerxes I, would restore outer strength. Hearing from relatives that Jerusalem's walls lay broken and its gates burned, Nehemiah's heart broke. He wept and fasted, praying, "Please, *Adonai*, let Your ear be attentive and Your eyes open, to hear the prayer of Your servant . . . We have acted very corruptly against You." (Nehemiah 1:6-7)

Granted permission and resources by the king, Nehemiah traveled to Jerusalem, surveyed the ruins by night, and rallied the people with faith's cry. "Come, let us rebuild the wall of Jerusalem, so that we will no longer be a disgrace." (Nehemiah 2:17)

Despite ridicule, conspiracies, and threats of attack, the builders labored with astonishing determination. Each held a sword in one hand and a trowel in the other. These actions demonstrated a vivid symbol of physical defense and spiritual perseverance. (Nehemiah 4:11)

Every gate repaired and every section completed became an act of prayer turned into masonry. In just fifty-two days the walls stood strong again. Nehemiah's leadership fused strategy with spirituality. His guidance provided steady organization interlaced with worship and fasting. His journal reads like a manual for holy resilience amid opposition.

After completion, the city's spiritual awakening blossomed. Ezra read aloud from the *Torah* from dawn until midday while the people stood, listening attentively. [13] As he blessed *Adonai*, the assembly responded, "Amen, Amen!" with lifted hands (Nehemiah 8:6). Many wept as they grasped the meaning of the words. However, the governor encouraged them differently, "Do not grieve, for the joy of *Adonai* is your strength." (Nehemiah 8:10) That statement distilled the entire Second Temple's mission that joy, not despair, would sustain their future.

---

[13] Ezra's public reading of the scroll in Nehemiah 8 functioned as a catalytic moment that helped define Judaism for the Second Temple period. Standing on a wooden platform, Ezra read the *Torah* aloud, with Levites translating and explaining so the people could understand, marking a shift toward text-centered, didactic worship rather than temple ritual alone. This event modeled regular public proclamation of *Torah*, which later developed into synagogue lectionary practice and established the Pentateuch as authoritative scripture for the community. The covenant renewal that followed—confession of sin, acceptance of specific laws, and communal commitment—reoriented Judean identity around obedience to written *Torah* as the primary marker of faithfulness in a post-exilic world without monarchy or prophecy. In this way, Ezra's reading helped create a shared scriptural norm that shaped *halakhic* development, sectarian debates, and Jewish self-understanding throughout the Second Temple era.

Worship Restored: Fire Rekindled on Zion

With the Temple rebuilt and the city fortified, worship flourished again. Music returned to the courts. Levites led choirs accompanied by cymbals, harps, and lyres. Psalms once birthed in exile now echoed off Jerusalem's resurrected stones.

The sacrifices resumed according to *Torah* command yet seasoned with lessons exile had taught. No longer was worship taken for granted. Every offering carried gratitude. "This was none other than the Lord's doing; it is marvelous in our eyes." (Psalm 118:23)

Rebuilding also required social justice. Nehemiah insisted that wealthy Judeans stop oppressing poorer neighbors through usury. Debts were canceled, servants freed, and equity restored. All provided proof that holiness cannot thrive while injustice festers (Nehemiah 5:1-13).

Feasts punctuated the rhythm of renewal. The people celebrated *Sukkot* with exuberance unmatched since the days of Joshua son of Nun (Nehemiah 8:17). Joy overflowed, not from perfection, but from restored relationship.

When they dedicated the wall, two great choirs marched in opposite directions around the city, meeting at the Temple in harmony. Trumpets blared as offered sacrifices smoked, "The joy of Jerusalem could be heard from far away." (Nehemiah 12:43)

This was more than noise. It was testimony that after centuries of exile, *Adonai*'s faithfulness had turned mourning into dancing. The physical restoration of Jerusalem mirrored spiritual truths still relevant for every believer.

1. Restoration begins with permission from heaven but requires participation from earth. Cyrus's decree opened the door, yet Israel had to walk through it in faith. God authors redemption, but His people must respond.

2. Renewal starts at the altar, not the walls. The exiles built an altar before anything else because worship precedes work. In personal faith, returning to first love comes before undertaking great projects.

3. Discouragement is part of every divine commission. Like Zerubbabel, believers encounter opposition from without and apathy within. The prophetic word, "Not by might" still reminds the weary that divine purpose triumphs *by Ruach*, not by resources.

4. Word and community sustain spiritual walls. Ezra's reading of *Torah* re-anchored the people in truth, while communal response sealed accountability. Modern discipleship likewise relies on shared Scripture and shared life.

5. Joy is both fruit and fortress. "The joy of *Adonai* is your strength" was no slogan. Rather, it was survival theology. Joy rooted in covenant sustains work under pressure.

Prophetic Echoes and Messianic Hints

The Second Temple's story carried forward Messianic undercurrents felt throughout Jewish expectation. Haggai foretold a greater glory yet to come, "The latter glory of this House will be greater than the former . . . and in this place I will give *shalom*." (Haggai 2:9)

The people wondered how could the new, smaller Temple ever rival Solomon's? The answer awaited fulfillment in the presence of Messiah Himself, who centuries later would walk its courts. His teaching, healing, and self-offering would embody the "greater glory" not of gold but of *Ruach Elohim* dwelling bodily among humankind.

Thus, the rebuilding era not only restored ancient worship but it prepared Israel's heart for the coming of the Redeemer. Covenant renewal after exile set the stage for ultimate redemption after sin.

A People Shaped by the Journey

By the time Nehemiah's reforms ended, Israel had become a transformed people. No longer defined solely by land or monarchy, they were shaped by Scripture, community, and hope.

Out of exile they had brought portable holiness, in restoration they rooted that holiness again to place and rhythm. The Temple, synagogue, and *Torah* study became three cords woven into one resilient faith.

Through persecution and dispersion that would follow under later empires, these patterns ensured survival. The same structure later nurtured a world fluent in prayer, fasting, and expectation of divine visitation into which *Yeshua* was born.

Lessons for the Pilgrim Heart

The story of return offers spiritual architecture for every generation emerging from seasons of exile, disappointment, or failure.

1. God's timing redeems delays. The seventy years of waiting were not lost time but preparatory grace. What feels like delay may be divine design for deeper dependence.

2. Rebuilding requires teamwork between leaders and laity. Zerubbabel, *Yehoshua*, Ezra, and Nehemiah each played distinct roles. Restoration flourishes when vision, worship, teaching, and administration operate together.

3. Sacred work needs both trowel and sword. Builders must guard their progress with prayer and vigilance. Spiritual warfare accompanies every advance of righteousness.

4. Walls matter as much as altars. Ethical, moral, and communal boundaries protect the worship restored at the center.

5. Joy sanctifies labor. The record ends not with exhaustion but celebration. To dedicate work through joy is to echo heaven's own rhythm of creation and rest.

Each believer holds within the walls of the heart a temple where *Adonai* desires to dwell. Sin, sorrow, or neglect may tear those walls down, but His decree of return still rings today, "Whoever belongs to My people, let him go up."

Perhaps you are living through your own spiritual exile. A season when enthusiasm has cooled or circumstances scattered your focus. A path back mirrors the ancient pattern:

1. Hear the decree. Recognize that release begins when God's word stirs your heart.
2. Rebuild the altar first. Rekindle prayer and worship before fixing externals.
3. Face opposition faithfully. Expect resistance but wield both sword (Scripture) and trowel (perseverance).
4. Let joy be strength. Celebrate every small victory. Allow gratitude to build endurance.
5. Dedicate the wall. Mark completion by thanksgiving so that praise concludes every project God begins.

As Jerusalem's stones rose from ruin, so too can faith rise from failure. The same *Ruach* that revived a nation rebuilds souls today. Each act of repentance and each word of Scripture embraced, adds a stone to the spiritual wall that protects communion with God.

When Nehemiah's choirs circled the city, their voices proclaimed the impossible made real. Covenant restored and presence renewed. Likewise, when believers lift songs after trial, heaven hears again "the joy of Jerusalem."

Epilogue to the Chapter: From Rubble to Radiance

The Second Temple period began with ashes and ended with anticipation. The people rebuilt what Babylon had broken. Yet beyond the mortar of their efforts gleamed a prophetic light. Through this restoration, *Adonai* demonstrated that His mercy outlives judgment, His promises outlast empires, and His faithfulness transcends every fall. "Those who sow in tears will reap with a song of joy. He who goes out weeping, carrying his seed-bag, will surely come again with a song of joy, carrying his sheaves." (Psalm 126:5-6)

The exiles had endured seventy years of hardship, but their perseverance bore fruit in the form of joy that served as a tangible testament to the power of hope in rebuilding even the most desolate of places. As we stand centuries later and read their story, the message remains unbroken. A message that a return is always possible, rebuilding is always grace, and the God who brought Israel home still calls each heart to rise and go up to Zion.

3

A People of the Book:
The Birth of Judaism

The Second Temple now stood gleaming in the sunlight on Mount Zion, a visible symbol that the exile's darkness had ended. Pilgrims again climbed to Jerusalem for *Pesach*, *Shavuot*, and *Sukkot*. In Jerusalem, incense rose, trumpets sounded, and priests served in their appointed courses. [14] Yet beneath the visible revival another, quieter revolution of a transformation deeper than architecture was taking place.

The destruction of Solomon's Temple and the seventy years of exile had not only toppled a city, but they had re-drawn Israel's spiritual map. Never again would worship depend solely on altar or monarchy. During the Persian and Hellenistic periods, Judaism began to take the shape recognizable today. It became a faith sustained by Scripture, study, community, and daily practice.

---

[14] *Shavuot*, the Feast of Weeks, is a major Jewish festival occurring seven weeks after Passover, marking the completion of the 49-day Counting of the Omer. Biblically, it is an agricultural celebration of the first wheat harvest and the bringing of the first fruits to the Temple in Jerusalem. Rabbinic tradition identifies Shavuot as the anniversary of the giving of the *Torah* and the Ten Commandments at Mount Sinai, when Israel fully became a covenant people bound by divine law. Contemporary observance emphasizes *Torah* study (often all-night learning), festive dairy meals, and synagogue readings of the Sinai narrative and the Book of Ruth. *Shavuot* thus weaves together themes of gratitude for physical sustenance, acceptance of spiritual responsibility, and renewed commitment to the covenant with God each year.

From this season emerged many of the features that still mark Jewish life. The synagogue, the Hebrew Scriptures as a defined canon, the oral teaching traditions, and an emphasis on ethics and learning became enshrined in the daily life of Israel. Israel became, in the words of later generations, "*Am HaSefer*," the People of the Book. "

The Rise of the Priests and Scribes

After the return from exile, the High Priesthood remained central to national identity. Yet the priestly role expanded beyond sacrifice. Priests became teachers of *Torah*. Malachi, writing in this period, reminded them, "For the lips of a *kohen* should guard knowledge, and instruction should be sought from his mouth, for he is a messenger of *Adonai-Tzva'ot*." (Malachi 2:7)

The priest's responsibility was no longer confined to ritual. The *Torah* that was once kept primarily in the Temple, now began traveling into villages and homes through scribes, or *soferim*. [15] These men meticulously copied the scrolls, preserving every letter with reverence. Each stroke became an act of worship.

---

[15] A scribe was a highly trained literate specialist who worked with texts, law, and administration at the heart of Jewish society. Many scribes were associated with the priesthood and Temple institutions, serving as copyists of Scripture, legal experts, and bureaucratic officials who drafted contracts, genealogies, and decrees. Their authority derived from mastery of the *Torah* and other traditions, so they taught, interpreted, and applied the law for both leaders and common people, functioning as judges, advisors, and teachers. Evidence suggests a spectrum: some were technical professional writers, while others formed an emerging intellectual class whose scriptural expertise shaped *halakhah* and communal norms, anticipating later rabbinic roles. In this way, scribes became key mediators between sacred texts, governing authorities, and daily Jewish life in the late Second Temple era.

As generations passed, the scribe took on even greater authority as interpreter and teacher. From their work came not only written accuracy but spiritual imagination. They grappled with the application of the *Torah* to everyday life. This included understanding how to observe *Shabbat* under Persian rule, how to tithe without relying on Levitical stores, and how to maintain purity among non-Jews. Through such reflection, the foundation of later rabbinic thought was laid.

Torah as the Heartbeat of Community

The *Torah* emerged as the constitution of Israel's renewed identity. In the absence of a king, it became the true sovereign. In the absence of national independence, it became the invisible boundary of holiness that no empire could erase.

Under Ezra and Nehemiah, the practice of public reading became institutionalized. Scripture records, "Ezra the *kohen* brought the *Torah* before the assembly — men, women and all who could listen with understanding — on the first day of the seventh month. He read from it . . . from early morning until midday." (Nehemiah 8:2-3) As Levites explained the meaning, people wept, not out of despair but conviction. The Word pierced deeper than any sword or exile. That day inaugurated the tradition of *Torah* reading in communal worship, a rhythm still practiced every *Shabbat* across the world.[16]

---

[16] *Shabbat*, the Jewish Sabbath, is the weekly day of sacred rest and celebration that begins at sunset on Friday and ends at nightfall on Saturday. The term *"Shabbat"* comes from the Hebrew root meaning "to cease" or "to rest," recalling God's resting after six days of

The shift was profound. Once, worshipers had gathered to present sacrifices performed by priests. Now they gathered to hear, study, and internalize God's Word. Holiness began to dwell in hearing and doing, not merely in offering and observing.

Learning became an act of love. Fathers taught sons the words of Deuteronomy 6. "These words, which I am commanding you today, are to be on your heart. You are to teach them diligently to your children and speak of them when you sit in your house, when you walk by the way, when you lie down and when you rise up." (Deuteronomy 6:6-7)

This daily engagement transformed education itself into a spiritual discipline. Studying was akin to worship, while memorizing was akin to drawing near to God. The very idea of *"Torah lishmah"* (learning for its own sake) to honor the Creator grew from this awakening.

From then onward, every home could become a miniature sanctuary. The table became the altar, the meal blessing became liturgy, and the family became a microcosm of Israel's covenant life.

The Synagogue: A New House for a Scattered People

As populations spread beyond Jerusalem, local assemblies formed to ensure that reading and prayer

---

creation. Biblically commanded in the Ten Commandments, it combines two core ideas: remembering God's creation and redemption from Egyptian slavery. *Shabbat* is marked by lighting candles before sunset, blessings over wine and bread (*kiddush* and *challah*), festive meals, prayer, and refraining from *melakhah*, categories of creative work. It functions as a weekly "sanctuary in time," offering joy, spiritual renewal, and dedicated time for family, study, and worship.

remained accessible. So emerged the synagogue (*beit knesset*, "house of gathering"). Its roots likely trace to Babylonian exile gatherings, but in the Second Temple era it matured into a structured institution.

Within synagogues, Israel encountered three innovations that would shape all subsequent faith:

1. Prayer as Sacrifice. Three daily prayer services *Shacharit* (morning), *Minchah* (afternoon), and *Ma'ariv* (evening) corresponding to the Temple's offerings. As Hosea had prophesied, "We will offer the bulls of our lips." (Hosea 14: 3) The spoken word became the new offering.

2. Scripture as Centerpiece. Scrolls were kept in an ark and read with reverence. The act of reading became performative theology and every service re-enacted Sinai.

3. Community as Covenant. The synagogue democratized the concept of holiness. It belonged not to priests alone but to entire communities. Anyone fluent in Scripture could read or comment, provided they spoke with humility before God's Word.

These gatherings sustained diaspora Jews long after the Temple's eventual fall. Indeed, by the first century CE synagogues existed throughout Judea, Galilee, Alexandria, and Asia Minor. Proof of spiritual portability that exile had taught.

Though sacrifices continued at the Second Temple until its destruction, their meaning was gradually reframed. The prophets had already prepared the way, "For I delight in mercy, not sacrifice, and knowledge of God more than burnt offerings." (Hosea 6:6) The focus shifted from ritual performance to ethical faithfulness. Psalmists and sages emphasized sincerity. "Who may dwell in Your tent? He who walks uprightly, who does what is right, and speaks truth in his heart." (Psalm 15:1-2)

Hence, obedience in daily conduct such as honest scales, compassion to the poor, and marital fidelity became the true liturgy of life. This transition did not abolish the Temple but internalized its purpose. The *korban* (offering) meant "drawing near" and the heart's repentance achieved what blood once symbolized. Centuries later, this principle would undergird *Yeshua*'s teaching when He declared, "Where your treasure is, there your heart will be also." (Luke 12:34)

In essence, the exile had burned away externals to reveal the true essence of relationship over ritual. That essence became the cornerstone of Judaism and, eventually, of Messianic faith itself.

The Psalms, Wisdom, and New Forms of Inspiration

During this creative age, Israel's spirituality found literary voice. Collections of psalms were organized, edited, and sung in the Second Temple. Wisdom writings like Proverbs, Job, and later Ecclesiastes were treasured as guides for practical holiness.

The Book of Chronicles was composed in the Persian era and retold Israel's history through a liturgical lens, highlighting priests, singers, and worship. Where the book of Kings ended in despair, Chronicles ended in hope with

Cyrus's decree. This was a deliberate signal that worship and obedience would carry the story forward.

In the same centuries, the seeds of apocalyptic literature (later blossoming in Daniel and *Enochic* writings) began to sprout. Visions of cosmic justice born from the experiences of oppression. These texts show a Judaism both rooted in *Torah* and reaching toward heaven while yearning for ultimate redemption.

The Formation of Canon and Tradition

Before exile, sacred writings circulated separately. *Torah* scrolls in priestly circles, prophetic scrolls among disciples, and psalms among musicians. During and after the Second Temple's early centuries, these texts were collected, copied, and revered as divinely inspired.

By the late Persian-Hellenistic period, the threefold division recognized in later Jewish tradition *Torah* (instruction), *Nevi'im* (prophets), and *Ketuvim* (writings) were taking shape.[17] Reading from these sections became customary in worship.

---

[17] The *Tanakh* is the canonical collection of Jewish sacred scriptures, often called the Hebrew Bible. It forms the foundational library of Israel's faith, story, and law, and is written primarily in biblical Hebrew with small portions in Aramaic. The word "Tanakh" itself is an acronym built from the names of its three major sections: *Torah*, *Nevi'im*, and *Ketuvim*. *Torah*, the "Law" or "Instruction," consists of the five books of Moses, which tell the story from creation through the Exodus and wilderness and present the core covenantal commandments. *Nevi'im*, the "Prophets," weaves together historical narratives and prophetic oracles that interpret Israel's history in light of covenant faithfulness and failure. *Ketuvim*, the "Writings," gathers poetry, wisdom, short narratives, and later histories such as Psalms, Proverbs, Ruth, and Chronicles. Together these three parts form the authoritative scriptural corpus for Judaism.

At the same time, oral teaching expanded as interpreters explained how written law applied to complex life. This living dialogue, the *Midrashic* instinct, kept revelation dynamic. It was not enough to preserve words. Additionally, the people sought to understand God's heartbeat within them. This synergy of written and oral *Torah*[18] would later blossom into the *Mishnah* and *Talmudic* tradition, but its roots lay within a community convinced that every letter carried eternity.

Daily Life as Holy Ground

Judaism, after the exile, became intensely practical. Where older Israelite religion had revolved around sacred times and places, the new Judaism sanctified everyday life.

- *Kashrut* (dietary laws) became an act of covenant identity.[19] Eating differently marked belonging.

---

[18] At this time in our story, "Oral *Torah*" is best described not yet as a formalized, named system, but as the living body of interpretive teaching, customs, and legal applications that surrounded the written *Torah* and guided its practice in new circumstances. As the Pentateuch crystallized as an authoritative text, priests, scribes, and later sages transmitted explanations, case rulings, and community norms by word of mouth—how to observe festivals, apply purity laws, conduct courts, and organize communal life—often extending or clarifying sparse written commands. These teachings circulated in schools, assemblies, and merging synagogue settings, and different groups (proto-Pharisees, priestly circles, later sects) developed distinctive interpretive traditions, already generating halakhic diversity and debate. In this early phase, Oral *Torah* functioned as dynamic, authoritative instruction attached to Moses' *Torah*, even before later rabbinic Judaism would explicitly define and name it as such.

[19] *Kashrut* described Israel's distinct dietary way of life, avoiding prohibited animals, blood, and certain fats, and shaping slaughter and food preparation. Keeping kosher visibly marked covenant identity and separation from surrounding peoples at table and in daily meals.

- *Tefillah* (prayer) structured the day, transforming work into worship breaks.
- *Tzedakah* (righteous giving) became as central as sacrifice, and caring for the poor mirrored God's own mercy.[20]
- *Mezuzot* [21] and *Tzitzit* [22] turned doorposts and garments into reminders of faith.

Thus, holiness moved from geography to rhythm and from institution to intention. The entire world became Temple ground for those who remembered the covenant.

This democratization of devotion was revolutionary. Every Jew whether priest or peasant, man or woman, near or far, could participate in the holy task of embodying *Torah*. The covenant community became not merely a nation under law, but a family living in wisdom.

---

[20] *Tzedakah* primarily expressed covenantal righteousness and justice rather than "charity" alone, rooted in *Torah* commands to protect the poor, widow, orphan, and stranger. Agricultural laws like gleanings, corners of fields, and remission of debts functioned as divinely mandated economic care, so support for the needy was seen as obeying God's just order, strengthening communal solidarity and defining Israel's ethical identity among surrounding peoples.

[21] *Mezuzot* were small parchment scrolls bearing passages from Deuteronomy, especially the Shema, affixed to doorposts in obedience to the command to write God's words on the doorposts of homes and gates. Archaeological finds from Qumran and other Judean sites show that by this time the practice was already established, making the *mezuzah* a visible sign of covenant loyalty and a daily reminder of God's presence and commandments at the threshold of Jewish dwellings.

[22] *Tzitzit* were specially knotted fringes attached to the four corners of Israelites' outer garments in obedience to Numbers 15:37–41 and Deuteronomy 22:12. Worn on everyday clothing rather than a separate ritual garment, these tassels often included a thread of blue (*tekhelet*) and served as a constant visual reminder to remember and keep all of God's commandments, marking Israel as a holy people set apart and signaling covenant identity within broader ancient Near Eastern society.

Persian tolerance allowed Judea self-governance under the High Priest and Elders. But when Alexander the Great conquered the Near East (332 BCE), the Greek language and worldview swept across the land. Hellenistic culture prized reason, beauty, and multiplicity of gods. These values both challenged and enriched Jewish identity. Out of this encounter came new developments:

- Translation. The *Torah* was rendered into Greek (the Septuagint) so diaspora Jews could read it.[23] This act preserved Scripture but also extended its reach to Gentile sympathizers, later called God-fearers.

- Wisdom literature engaged philosophical questions about virtue, fate, and free will (as seen in later books like Ben Sira).

- Apocalyptic hope intensified under persecution, expressing trust that God would vindicate His people. This became a precursor to Messianic expectation.

Through it all, one conviction remained immovable: *Adonai* is One. No pantheon, king, or philosopher could replace the confession of the *Shema in* Deuteronomy 6:4, "Hear O Israel, *Adonai* our God, *Adonai* is One."[24] That

---

[23] The Septuagint, often abbreviated LXX, is the earliest surviving Greek translation of the Hebrew Scriptures, produced for Greek-speaking Jews, especially in Egypt, beginning in the third century BCE. According to tradition, about seventy Jewish scholars first translated the *Torah* in Alexandria, with the remaining books rendered over the following century or two. The Septuagint includes all books of the Hebrew Bible plus additional works later called Apocrypha or Deuterocanonical by various Christian traditions.

[24] For Jews in the early Second Temple period, the *Shema* of Deuteronomy 6:4–5 functioned as a central confession of Israel's allegiance to the one God of Israel and to covenant obedience. Recited regularly and associated with Temple liturgy, it affirmed

steadfast devotion upheld identity through every cultural storm and laid theological ground for both Rabbinic monotheism and early Messianic faith.

Spiritual Innovation and Ethical Emphasis

As the faith matured, moral vision deepened. Prophets like Zechariah and Malachi linked ritual purity with social justice. Later teachers stressed that true worship demanded ethical integrity.

Rabbinic sources would later phrase it, "The world stands on three things: *Torah*, *Avodah* (worship), and *Gemilut Chasadim* (acts of kindness)." This triple cord was establishing study, prayer, and compassion as the essence of faith. While the exile had taught dependence, restoration taught responsibility. To know the covenant was to embody its compassion. Thus, Judaism evolved into a practical holiness. It became a faith of doing justly, loving mercy, and walking humbly with One's God. (Micah 6:8)

In the emerging community, families became key transmitters of faith. Women, who sustained identity in exile, continued to teach prayer, observe dietary laws, and light Sabbath lamps. Their role at home paralleled the priest's role in the Temple as guardians of sanctity within domestic walls.

The home became a *mikdash me'at*, a "little sanctuary." Around its table blessings were spoken, psalms recited,

---

that the Lord alone was Israel's God in a world of many deities, marking Jewish identity through exclusive loyalty to *Adonai*. The *Shema* also bound love of God to daily life—teaching children, binding words on hand and head, inscribing them on homes—so that monotheistic faith shaped home, memory, and communal practice from morning to night.

and wine sanctified. This household spirituality fortified Judaism against any future dispersion, as wherever a Jewish home stood, Zion continued to exist.

The Scroll and the Spirit

By the late Second Temple period, a new image of a people holding the scroll defined Israel. In art, prayer, and imagination, the *Torah* became almost personified as a source of wisdom speaking through every generation. Psalm 19 celebrated this identity, "The *Torah* of *Adonai* is perfect, restoring the soul. The testimony of *Adonai* is sure, making the simple wise . . . More desirable than gold, yes, more than much pure gold." (Psalm 19:8, 11)

The Word that once thundered at Sinai now whispered from parchment, yet its power had not diminished. It taught that God reveals Himself not only through wonders and fire, but through letters carefully inked and faithfully kept.

This reverence for revelation birthed enduring customs such as standing when a *Torah* scroll is lifted, kissing it as it passes, and wrapping it in beauty. As Jeremiah had promised long ago, "I will put My *Torah* within them. Yes, I will write it on their heart." (Jeremiah 31:32) The written scroll on earth mirrored the inscription upon the soul.

The Birth of Judaism: A Summary of Newness

By the close of the Persian and early Hellenistic eras, Israel had become something new yet ancient. It was a faith refashioned by fire, text, and time. Key innovations included:

- Scriptural Canon. *Torah*, Prophets, and Writings (*Tanakh*) was recognized as inspired authority.
- Synagogue Worship. Decentralized prayer and study were accepted as alternatives to sacrifice.
- Daily Piety. Prayer services, blessings, and ethical commandments were integrated into routine life.
- Scribal Scholarship. The emergence of interpretive schools transmitted both written and oral teaching.
- Universal Monotheism. Adonai's rule was affirmed over all nations, not just a tribal territory, and His majesty was ascribed.
- Hope of Redemption. Apocalyptic and Messianic expectation evolved from prophetic promise.

In short, exilic trauma had metamorphosed into creative theology. The loss of one center produced countless centers, until every community, every home, and every heart could host the Presence.

When centuries later *Yeshua* taught in Galilee's synagogues and debated scribes in Jerusalem, He stepped into this world that the Babylonian exile had fashioned. His message of the Kingdom drew upon *Torah*, prophets, and prayer patterns born in the very age we have traced.

He quoted Deuteronomy and Psalms, taught mercy above ritual, and gathered disciples to study and live the Word. Thus continuing, not discarding, Second Temple Judaism's deepest insight that God longs for hearts inscribed with His teaching. His followers were Jewish men and women steeped in scripture, prayer, and ethical vision who would carry that tradition outward to the nations, showing that the covenant message born in

Babylon and refined in Persia was destined for global fulfillment.

Reflection: Living as People of the Book

The story of this chapter invites self-examination. We, too, are called to be *ha-sefer*, bearers of divine wisdom. Do we read Scripture as living voice or mere history? Have we made our homes sanctuaries of prayer and study? Do we honor God by acts of justice as much as words of praise?

Judaism's birth out of exile proves that faith does not die when circumstances change. Rather, it evolves into maturity. Babylon may burn the Temple but cannot silence the Word. Empires may rule the land but cannot conquer the soul that delights in *Torah*. "Your word is a lamp to my feet and a light to my path." (Psalm 119:105)

That lamp still shines. Every generation that tends its flame joins the unbroken chain first kindled by Ezra's scrolls and the scribes who copied them. We, too, must become living scrolls having hearts inscribed with the covenant, and our lives declaring that the Word of *Adonai* endures forever.

4

When Greece Came East: The Challenge of Hellenism

Only a few generations after the return from Babylon, a new storm gathered over the horizon. This challenge was not of chariots from the east, but of phalanxes from the west. In 334 BCE, Alexander the Great crossed the Hellespont, leading an army that carried not only weapons but a worldview. By the time of his death eleven years later, his empire reached from Greece to India.[25]

Jerusalem and Judea lay between those giants Persia and Egypt, directly in Alexander's path. Unlike Babylon or Persia, the Greeks did not primarily seek to destroy or displace. Rather, their mission was to transform. Hellenism was not merely a political rule. It was a culture, a language, and a way of seeing the world.

To many nations, Greek civilization appeared irresistibly beautiful. It offered art, architecture, philosophy, and a vision of human excellence celebrated in the gymnasium and marketplace. Yet beneath its shining marble ran the subtle threat of a temptation to measure truth by human wisdom rather than divine revelation.

---

[25] Arrian, *Anabasis of Alexander*, trans. P. A. Brunt (Cambridge: Harvard University Press, Loeb), 1:3–11; Robin Lane Fox, *Alexander the Great* (London: Penguin, 2004), 85–92.

For the people of Israel, this encounter would become the defining test of the Second Temple era. Could they engage Greek culture without compromising covenant? Could *Torah*-faith survive amid the glitter of Athens?

Alexander's Empire and God's Providence

Jewish storytellers later preserved a legend that when Alexander approached Jerusalem, the High Priest Jaddua met him in priestly robes. Seeing him, Alexander bowed, saying he had dreamed of such a man before his eastern campaigns. [26] Whether legend or layered memory, the story reflects the truth that even in the swirl of world conquest, *Adonai*'s providence ruled history.

For centuries Persia had dominated Judea, now the map shifted overnight. Alexander's policy of respect toward local faiths allowed the Jews relative peace. They were granted freedom to follow their ancestral laws and continued temple worship unhindered. But the true legacy of Alexander was not tolerance but language. *Koine Greek* became the common speech of empire, linking marketplaces and scholars from Egypt to Mesopotamia. Now, for the first time since Babel, a single tongue connected the world. Into that shared vocabulary, both Jewish and later Christian thought would transfer revelation through a common language.

---

[26] Josephus, Flavius *Antiquities of the Jews*, trans. H. St. J. Thackeray (Cambridge: Harvard University Press, Loeb), 6:370–391.

The Spread of Hellenism

After Alexander's death in 323 BCE, his generals divided the empire, birthing rival kingdoms. Judea found itself wedged between two: the Ptolemies ruling from Alexandria in Egypt and the Seleucids ruling from Antioch in Syria. For more than a century, Judea oscillated between their control like a pawn in a cosmic chess game.[27]

Under Ptolemaic rule (323–198 BCE), Jewish life generally prospered. The most striking development occurred in Alexandria, where a vast Jewish population embraced the Greek language wholeheartedly. There, around the third century BCE, seventy or seventy-two scholars produced a Greek translation of the *Torah* known as the Septuagint (LXX). The Septuagint was a monumental work that would later shape the vocabulary of the New Covenant Scriptures.

For diaspora Jews, the Septuagint became the bridge by which exile communities retained faith while living in a Greek world. Yet its very creation posed new questions. If the Word of God could be spoken in Greek, could its meaning also cross cultures? Did divine truth depend upon the Hebrew tongue, or could the nations hear in their own words? Already the seeds of universal mission lay hidden within translation.

But Hellenism's spread was double-edged. Greek education promoted ideals of beauty and rational pursuit that often clashed with covenant ethics. Gymnasiums,

---

[27] Koester, Craig R. "Judea during Hellenistic Rule (332 BCE–165 BCE)." Enter the Bible. Luther Seminary, July 19, 2021. Accessed April 4, 2026. https://enterthebible.org/time-period/judea-during-hellenistic-rule/.

theaters, and festivals celebrated human form and polytheistic myth. Statues of gods and heroes filled cities. For observant Jews, such imagery violated the first commandments.[28]

In Judea itself, Hellenistic customs began to seep inward. Wealthy families dressed in Greek style, gave their children Greek names, and admired Greek philosophy. Some young men even underwent painful medical procedures to hide the mark of circumcision, a symbol of shame before their new peers. Once again, Israel faced the ancient temptation to be like the nations.

The conflict between *Torah* and Hellenism was more than cultural preference. Instead, it was a battle for the soul's allegiance. Greek thought centered humanity at the universe's core while *Torah* placed *Adonai* there.

Greek wisdom taught that divinity lay within the natural order. Within that order, gods were born of chaos, sharing form with creation itself.[29] The God of Israel declared the opposite, "I am *Adonai*, that is My Name; My glory I will not give to another." (Isaiah 42:8)

Greek ethics sought moderation while *Torah* demanded holiness. Greek art worshiped the human body, but *Torah* engraved holiness upon the body through covenant signs. Greek philosophy celebrated reason and debate conflicting with *Torah*'s required humble obedience to revelation. To live faithfully in a Hellenistic world therefore demanded spiritual discipline and creative resilience.

---

[28] Hadas, Moses. "Judaism and the Hellenistic Experience: A Classical Model for Living in Two Cultures." Commentary 42, no. 2 (1966): 93–101.

[29] Hesiod. Theogony. Translated by Glenn W. Most. Loeb Classical Library 57. Cambridge, MA: Harvard University Press, 2006.

Eleazar and His Influence

Ancient writings such as 2 Maccabees preserve stirring accounts of those who resisted assimilation. One legend tells of Eleazar, an elderly scholar ordered by Antiochus to eat pork, a public act renouncing *Torah*. He refused, choosing death rather than dishonor. His final words reportedly praised God, "It is fitting to suffer for the sake of our heavenly law." Such tales, though from later sources, convey the conviction that loyalty to *Adonai* must transcend life itself.

Meanwhile, other Jews sought the middle path of engaging Greek learning while remaining faithful. Books like Proverbs, Ben Sira (Ecclesiasticus), and later The Wisdom of Solomon reflect the synthesis of blending Hebrew revelation with philosophical reflection. Wisdom became the meeting place of cultures and promoted the idea that the Creator's order could be discerned in creation itself.

Ben Sira warned against arrogance before foreign thought, "The beginning of wisdom is the fear of *Adonai*" (Proverbs 9:10). Wisdom literature thus served as both bridge and boundary. It was open to learning but closed to idolatry. Out of this cultural collision emerged literary creativity unmatched since the prophets. Three developments stand out:

1. Apocalyptic Vision. As foreign powers rose and faith communities felt powerless, a new genre expressed hope through heavenly visions. The Book of Daniel, set in earlier Babylonian exile yet written during the Hellenistic crisis, revealed a cosmic view of history. "The God of heaven will set up a kingdom

that will never be destroyed . . . It will crush and put an end to all these kingdoms, but it will itself endure forever." (Daniel 2:44)

Through such imagery, Jews reinterpreted history's turmoil as divine plan leading toward ultimate deliverance.

2. Expanded Angels and Afterlife. Interaction with Greek and Persian ideas prompted reflection on heavenly beings, resurrection, and judgment. Concepts glimpsed in Isaiah and Ezekiel blossomed into clearer hope that the righteous would awake to everlasting life (Daniel 12:2). Faith matured from national restoration to cosmic redemption.

3. The Philosophy of the Word. In Alexandria, Jewish thinkers like Philo would later merge Greek metaphysics with Hebrew theology, describing the *Logos* (Word) as God's instrument of creation. Though Philo lived centuries later, the intellectual soil for such synthesis was prepared in this era. The same term "Word" (*Logos*) would later become the centerpiece of the Gospel of John, "The Word became flesh." History was converging on revelation.

Despite cultural attraction, a remnant remained steadfast. Their motto could have been that of the psalmist, "Your word I have treasured in my heart, so that I might not sin against You." (Psalm 119:11) They clung to Scripture reading, Sabbath observance, and distinctive dress. Families taught children the lessons of covenant identity, "You are a chosen people . . . Who is a nation so great who has God so near as *Adonai* our God?" (Deuteronomy 4:7) Some scholars refer to this contrast as "the *Torah* party" versus "the Hellenist party," but these were not political factions so much as the spiritual orientations of faithfulness versus compromise, and revelation versus reason without God.[30]

It is vital to understand that not all of Hellenism was evil. Greek science, architecture, and language expanded human understanding, and God's truth would later travel its roads. Yet for every generation, the challenge of how to express eternal truth in contemporary culture without losing its essence remained.

Jerusalem under the Seleucids

Around 200 BCE the balance of power shifted again when the Seleucids wrested Judea from Ptolemaic rule. At first, King Antiochus III confirmed Jewish privileges. Within a few decades his descendant Antiochus IV Epiphanes, a man intoxicated by absolute power, sought to unify his realm through forced Hellenization. He outlawed circumcision, *Shabbat*, and *Torah* study. He erected idols in the Temple and desecrated its altar with pagan sacrifice (1 Maccabees 1:41-64). The event became known as the Abomination of Desolation (Daniel 11:31).

For the first time, Jewish identity faced eradication not merely through exile but through assimilation by decree.

---

[30] Collins, John J. *The Apocalyptic Imagination* (Grand Rapids: Eerdmans, 2016), 24–32, 56–65; Martin Hengel, *Judaism in the Hellenistic Age* (Philadelphia: Fortress Press, 1974), 72–80.

Faith had to choose between compromise and martyrdom. Out of this persecution rose the Maccabean revolt. This revolt was a heroic resistance that would restore the Temple, purify its altar, and inspire the feast of Hanukkah. That story will unfold in the next chapter, but its roots lie here, in the creeping compromise of Hellenism before persecution turned overt.

Lessons from Hellenistic Encounter

The Greek challenge brought both peril and providence. It threatened faith yet also refined and prepared it for global mission. Its lessons remain timely:

1. Cultural brilliance is not moral light. Wisdom without revelation easily becomes idolatry of reason.

2. Language can be a bridge for witness. The Greek tongue that once enticed assimilation later carried the message of Messiah to the nations.

3. Faith must discern, not withdraw. Isolation breeds ignorance while compromise breeds dilution. The faithful must engage culture while anchoring identity in *Torah* and Spirit.

4. Adversity births theology. Under the pressure of Hellenism, Israel developed deeper reflection on resurrection, judgment, and the hope of a coming Kingdom. These became the themes central to later Messianic faith.

5. God rules empires by purpose, not coincidence. Daniel saw that the succession of beasts and

kingdoms was guided by the Ancient of Days. History bends toward His decree.

Even as Greek marble crumbled and visionaries debated ethics, the prophets' word endured. "For the earth will be filled with the knowledge of the glory of *Adonai*, as the waters cover the sea." (Habakkuk 2:14)

No human philosophy could fulfill that promise; only embodied revelation could. Centuries later, the Gospel writers would write their messages in Greek. Yet their Greek content would proclaim the Hebrew God. What Hellenism intended for self-exaltation became the vessel of divine communication. Such irony reveals the hidden sovereignty of heaven.

Reflection: When Cultures Collide

Every believer stands at some crossroads between covenant and culture. Our modern world offers its own Greek temptations. Admiration for intellect without humility, beauty without holiness, and power without service. The question of how God's people shall live amid the lures of a global civilization remains unchanged.

The story of Hellenism teaches backbone and grace. God did not call His people to flee the world but to remain distinct within it. The faithful in Judea learned to walk through gymnasiums without bowing to idols, to speak Greek yet pray in Hebrew heart-language, and to employ wisdom yet fear *Adonai*.

So must we. The covenant remains countercultural, even when written in the empire's tongue. "Do not be conformed to this world, but be transformed by the renewing of your mind, so you may discern what is the

will of God — what is good and acceptable and perfect."
(Romans 12:2)

The Greeks built temples of marble to human glory. Israel built communities of faith to divine glory. In an age that still worships the self, we are summoned back to that ancient distinction, "Hear O Israel, *Adonai* is our God, *Adonai* is One."

When the philosophies of the world grow loud, may we remember the wisdom that never fades. "The fear of *Adonai* is the beginning of knowledge, but fools despise wisdom and discipline." (Proverbs 1:7)

Through exile, empire, and encounter, the people of the Book learned that truth does not fear reason. Nevertheless, reason must bow before Revelation. And when Greek light and Hebrew faith met upon history's stage, the groundwork was laid for a greater revelation. The light of Messiah, through whom both Jew and Gentile, would find true wisdom and everlasting life.

Part II: Foreign Kings and Faithful Hearts

5

War for the Holy Place: The Maccabees and Hanukkah

No generation is born into peace by accident. It must protect or rediscover it. The centuries after Alexander's conquest proved that cultural brilliance could mask moral corruption. Under his successors, the Seleucid kings, Judea's autonomy weakened, and the covenant was slowly squeezed between taxation and temptation.

By 175 BCE, pressure turned to persecution. Antiochus IV Epiphanes, ascending the Seleucid throne, styled himself "God Manifest." Where previous rulers tolerated diversity, this one demanded uniformity. To bind his empire, he sought to erase distinctions, including Israel's. His decrees struck at the heart of Jewish faith. Circumcision was banned. *Torah* scrolls were burned. *Shabbat* and festivals were outlawed. Offerings to pagan gods were required by law.[31]

Those who defied him were executed. Yet the crowning insult came in Jerusalem itself. In 167 BCE Antiochus entered the Holy City, plundered the Temple treasury, and erected on the altar an image of Zeus Olympias. He commanded that pigs, unclean animals under *Torah*, be

---

[31] Rappaport, Aharon. "What Motivated Antiochus to Issue His Decrees Against the Jews?" Hakirah: The Flatbush Journal of Jewish Law and Thought 16 (2013): 177–208.

sacrificed upon it, and that the Temple be rededicated to his god.[32]

The Book of Daniel had foreseen it centuries earlier, "Forces from him will arise, profane the sanctuary fortress, and abolish the daily offering. They will set up the abomination of desolation." (Daniel 11:31)

Smoke of defilement rose where incense once had. The chants of Hellenistic priests replaced psalms of David. To the faithful remnant, it felt as if creation itself were overturned. The covenant people who had endured exile now faced something worse than exile. They feared eradication. Yet even as darkness fell on Zion, divine purpose was kindling elsewhere.

Fifty miles northwest of Jerusalem lay the small town of Modiin, home to an aged priest named Mattathias *ben Yochanan*, descendant of Phinehas. When Antiochus's officers arrived, demanding that the people sacrifice to idols, Mattathias refused. "Even if all the nations within the king's dominion obey him and abandon the religion of their ancestors, yet I and my sons and my brothers will continue to follow the covenant of our fathers. Heaven forbid that we should forsake the *Torah* and commandments." (1 Maccabees 2:19-21)

When an apostate Jew stepped forward to comply, Mattathias' zeal erupted. He struck down both the officer and the traitor, tore down the idol altar, and cried to the crowd, "All who are zealous for *Torah* and maintain the covenant—follow me!" With his five sons, Yohanan,

---

[32] 1 Maccabees 1:20–24, 54–59; 2 Maccabees 6:1–5; Flavius Josephus, H. St. J. Thackeray, 7:326–333.

Shimon, Eleazar, Jonathan, and Judah, he fled into the hills. The flame of resistance was lit.

From small bands of fugitives, the Hasmonean revolt began. Their hiding places in the Judean wilderness became schools of faith and warfare. They attacked royal outposts by night, shattered pagan altars, circumcised infants, and restored *Torah* observance wherever they advanced. Mattathias did not live to see victory. On his deathbed he charged his sons, "Be zealous for the *Torah* and give your lives for the covenant of your fathers. Remember the deeds of our ancestors." (1 Maccabees 2:50–51)

Leadership passed to his third son, Judah, soon known as *HaMaccabi*, "the Hammer." His courage inspired trembling farmers to stand like lions. Their prayer echoed Moses' cry at the Red Sea. "It is easy for many to be given into the hands of few; victory in battle does not depend on numbers but on strength from heaven." (1 Maccabees 3:18–19)

Equipped with faith, not armor, Judah's army struck Seleucid forces in ambush at Emmaus and other battles. Enemy generals mocked the guerrillas as rustic rebels until their disciplined faith overcame imperial might. Each victory rekindled belief that *Adonai* still fought for His people, as in days of Gideon and David.

The Cleansing of the Temple

By 165 BCE, after three years of struggle, Judah captured Jerusalem. He found ivy garlands carved along the Temple walls, swine bones on the altar, and idols within the court. The defilement was total. Judah's first act was purification. The soldiers wept aloud, tore garments, and threw themselves upon the ground. Then, under the high priest *Yohanan* and the Levites, they removed the defiled stones to a separate place, built a new altar, and crafted holy vessels anew.

On the twenty-fifth day of *Kislev* in the one-hundred-forty-eighth year (164 BCE), they offered the first lawful sacrifice on the new altar. Exactly three years to the day since it had been desecrated. Trumpets sounded while cymbals clashed. The people fell on their faces and blessed the God of heaven, crying out the words of the Psalms, "Give thanks to *Adonai*, for He is good, for His lovingkindness endures forever!" (Psalm 118:1)

The rededication lasted eight days perhaps recalling *Sukkot*, which persecution had prevented them from keeping. The joy was so great that Judah and his brothers decreed the festival should be kept every year in perpetuity. Thus *Hanukkah*, or "Dedication," was born. (1 Maccabees 4)

Centuries later, rabbinic tradition added a tender detail. Upon re-entering the Temple, the priests found only one sealed flask of pure oil, enough to light the *menorah* for a single day. They lit it nonetheless, and the flame burned eight days until new oil could be prepared.[33] Whether miracle of oil or miracle of victory, the meaning endures and the light refuses to die. The *menorah* became a symbol

---

[33] The Babylonian *Talmud*: Tractate *Shabbat*. Translated by I. Epstein. London: Soncino Press, 1938. *Shabbat* 21b.

of hope through generations.[34] Even the smallest spark, blessed by God, can outshine empires.

At every *Hanukkah* since, Jews light candles in windows, declaring that darkness never triumphs. The exiled repeatedly have looked upon those flames as proof that history bends toward redemption.

For followers of *Yeshua*, the feast echoes deeper still. The Gospel records Him observing the Feast of Dedication in Jerusalem. (John 10:22–23) There, amid the winter chill, He spoke, "I am the Light of the world."[35] The same God who preserved the *menorah's* flame embodied divine light in flesh.

Freedom and Fallout: The Hasmonean Kingdom

The Maccabean revolt secured more than Temple purification. It birthed a century of Jewish self-rule and the Hasmonean Kingdom. Judah's brothers Jonathan and Simon expanded boundaries, minted coins, and negotiated

---

[34] The *Hanukkah menorah*, or *hanukkiah*, is a nine-branched candelabrum developed to commemorate the rededication of the Jerusalem Temple after the Maccabean victory in 164 BCE. Eight branches represent the eight days of celebration, recalling the tradition that a single day's supply of consecrated oil miraculously burned for eight days when the Temple *menorah* was relit. The ninth branch, the *shamash* ("servant"), is used to kindle the others and is set apart in height or position. In the early post-Maccabean Second Temple context, *Hanukkah* lights symbolized renewed covenant fidelity and divine help, echoing the Temple menorah's imagery of God's presence while shifting that light into homes and public spaces to mark Jewish identity under ongoing foreign rule.

[35] *Yeshua's* presence in the Temple at the Feast of Dedication and His claim, "I am the Light of the world," gather *Hanukkah's* themes of preserved light, covenant fidelity, and renewed sanctuary into Himself, presenting Him as the embodied, enduring light that no foreign power, spiritual darkness, or defilement can extinguish.

with foreign powers. For the first time since Zedekiah, Judea tasted sovereignty.

At first, zeal for *Torah* guided the government. The people saw in the Maccabees fulfillment of the psalmist's prayer, "Some trust in chariots, and some in horses, but we will trust in the Name of *Adonai* our God." (Psalm 20:8) Yet power carries peril. As the dynasty flourished, politics began to eclipse piety. Hasmonean rulers adopted Greek titles and engaged in regional power struggles. Priests became princes, and their zeal hardened into factionalism. Throughout these decades, the spiritual movements of the Pharisees, the Sadducees, and the Essenes were strengthened. Pharisees emphasized personal holiness and oral interpretation of *Torah*. The Sadducees, drawn from the priestly elite, prioritized Temple ritual and cooperation with rulers. Eventually, the Essenes withdrew to wilderness purity.[36]

The diversity of thought born from freedom would both enrich and divide Israel. But the memory of Judah Maccabee's courage continued to inspire hope that God raises deliverers in every generation.

Hanukkah's Theology of Perseverance

Hanukkah is more than a tale of liberation. Rather, it is theology written in firelight.

1. Holiness Can Be Rebuilt. The Temple, once profaned, could be cleansed and rededicated. So too the human heart, our inner sanctuary, though

---

[36] 1 Maccabees 13:36–42; Flavius Josephus, H. St. J. Thackeray, 7:364–515; Hengel, Martin. *Judaism in the Hellenistic Age* (Philadelphia: Fortress Press, 1974), 288–298.

defiled by compromise, can be made pure again through repentance and grace. The story shouts the truth of Joel 2:13, "Tear your heart, not your garments, and turn to *Adonai* your God, for He is gracious and compassionate."

2. Few with God Outnumber Many without Him.

    The Maccabees were skilled but small. Faith tipped the scales. Their victories illustrate Zechariah's timeless promise, "Not by might, nor by power, but by *My Ruach*." (Zechariah 4:6)

3. Light Is Meant to Be Seen. Jewish law later required *Hanukkah* lamps to be placed where passersby could see them known as *pirsumei nissa*, "publicizing the miracle."[37] Faith is not private survival but visible witness. As *Yeshua* said, "No one lights a lamp and puts it under a basket." (Matthew 5:15)

4. Victory Demands Vigilance. The same family that won freedom later wrestled with pride. Every spiritual triumph carries temptation to self-glory. Dedication must be renewed daily, not celebrated once.

The Maccabean revolt reverberated far beyond Judea. Regional powers observed in awe: a small theocratic nation defying empire and winning. While rising on the western horizon, Roman senators sent envoys establishing friendly treaties with Judah's successors, recognizing shared admiration for perseverance and freedom.

---

[37] The Babylonian *Talmud, Shabbat* 21b.

Politically, the Hasmonean state became a buffer between conquering empires. Spiritually, it proclaimed to surrounding nations that fidelity to one God could outlast idols and armies. The candles of *Hanukkah* burned as a declaration of divine sovereignty amid human politics.

Within two centuries, Rome would dominate Judea, and once again foreign rule would test faith. Yet the memory of the Maccabees lingered, nourishing expectations of future deliverance. This deliverance would manifest through a Messiah who would liberate not just the Temple precincts but the human soul. The cry, "God has delivered us before; He will do so again!" became the soil of first-century Messianic hope.

Hidden Light: The Hanukkah Pattern in Every Age

Hanukkah's pattern of desecration, devotion, and divine deliverance repeats throughout history. Each generation's "Antiochus" may take new forms like tyranny, assimilation, and cynicism. However, the covenant pattern endures. Desecration is anything that replaces God's glory with human pride. Devotion is the decision to stand, altarless if need be, to honor His Name. Deliverance is the moment His light returns, proving darkness is temporary.

Believers, Jewish and Gentile alike, across the centuries relate to this rhythm. In every revival, in every rediscovery of the Word after neglect, the spirit of *Hanukkah* is reborn. "Though I sit in darkness, *Adonai* is my light." (Micah 7:8) The *menorah* burning in exile became the world's testimony that God still writes transfiguration into tragedy.

Rabbinic sages prescribed the lighting of additional candles each night. One the first evening, two the next, and finally culminating in eight. Why increase light rather than decrease, as others suggested? Because in divine economy, holiness grows brighter with time. Every act of faith should magnify, not diminish, illumination. The *Talmud* declared, "We ascend in holiness; we do not descend."[38] That principle mirrors the very essence of spiritual growth. Each obedient act or deed ignites a flame within, gradually transforming the entire life into a radiant beacon of hope.

Yeshua captured this same principle, "The path of the righteous is like the light of dawn, shining ever brighter until full day." (Proverbs 4:18). Thus, the *menorah* is not only remembrance but roadmap showing that faith enhances brightness daily through steadfast devotion.

Lighting *Hanukkah* candles, then, is an annual rededication of the inner sanctuary. We pause before the flickering light and whisper, "Lord, cleanse my temple again. Rekindle what compromise has dimmed." In that simple act, ancient history becomes immediate covenant.

Historical Reflections: Between Legend and Legacy

Modern historians differentiate legend from verifiable fact, yet both matter for theology. The Hasmonean revolt unquestionably occurred and archaeological and textual evidence confirm it. Whether or not oil truly lasted eight days, the perceived miracle carried equally enduring impact. For the people of faith, miracles are not suspensions of nature but revelations of meaning. The oil

---

[38] The Babylonian *Talmud*, *Shabbat* 21b.

story crystallized a larger truth that God multiplies limited devotion into limitless testimony. One sanctified lamp defied darkness. So does each life set apart for Him.

Even critics who view *Hanukkah* politically must concede its spiritual resonance. A festival without imperial sanction that does not celebrates conquest of nations, but rather, purification of worship. It sanctifies resistance to spiritual erosion an idea that is relentlessly relevant.

Hanukkah's imagery of light in darkness, dedication after defilement, and deliverance through zeal became prophetic language pointing toward Messianic redemption. Later Jewish mystics saw in its eight lights a symbol of eternity, one beyond the seven-day perfection of creation. The eighth day hints at new creation, just as the Maccabean victory hinted at ultimate restoration.

When *Yeshua* declared, "I am the Light of the world" during the Feast of Dedication, He was not introducing novelty. Rather, He was revealing fulfillment. The same God who purified the altar now purified humanity. As *Hanukkah* commemorated cleansing from idolatry, so His ministry cleansed hearts to become living temples of *Ruach HaKodesh*.

Thus, for Messianic believers, *Hanukkah's* flames recall both history and hope. The past light that conquered night will again emerge when "the glory of *Adonai* will rise upon you." (Isaiah 60:1)

Lessons from the Hammer

Judah Maccabee's courage teaches enduring leadership principles:

1. Conviction before Consensus. He acted while others debated. Faith begins where fear ends.

2. Holiness Requires Action. The altar could not cleanse itself. Someone had to strike the match of obedience.

3. Zeal Tempered by Humility. The hammer that breaks idols must remain guided by gentleness toward fellow strugglers. Zeal without wisdom corrodes what it defends.

4. Remembrance Sustains Resistance. The Maccabees fought remembering Abraham, Moses, and David. Likewise, every believer stands by recollection of God's past faithfulness.

Two millennia later, Jewish homes around the world still kindle lights each *Kislev*, reciting, "Blessed are You, *Adonai* our God, King of the universe, who performed miracles for our ancestors in those days at this season."[39] Children spin the *dreidel*, a playful echo of hidden learning in times when public *Torah* study was forbidden.[40] On each *dreidel*, the four Hebrew letters of Nun, *Gimel, Hey, Shin* form the phrase "*Nes Gadol Hayah Sham*" ("A Great Miracle Happened There"). In Israel, the last letter changes *to Pey*

---

[39] "Blessings for Lighting the Hanukkah Candles." In Hanukkah: Blessings and Readings. HIAS, 2020. PDF, 1.

[40] A *dreidel* is a four-sided spinning top used in a traditional Hanukkah game, usually made of wood or plastic and marked with the Hebrew letters *nun, gimel, hey,* and *shin,* an acronym for "a great miracle happened there." To play, each person starts with an equal number of tokens (such as coins or candy) and puts one into a central pot. Players take turns spinning the *dreidel*; when it stops, the top face determines the action: *nun* means do nothing, *gimel* take the whole pot, *hey* take half, and *shin* put one token into the pot. The game continues with players alternating turns until one person has won all the tokens or participants decide to stop.

for "*Po*" ("here") declaring that the miracle was not distant but local, and eternal by extension.

Hanukkah's rhythm fills winter darkness with communal warmth. It unites families around gratitude rather than despair. Even without Temple or king, every window light proclaims Israel's unbroken story that God is still here.

Reflection: Rededication for the Rest of Us

Standing before the eighth light, every believer hears a silent invitation to dedicate again. Where have idols of habits, fears, and divided loyalties crept into our own Holy Place? *Hanukkah* calls us to cleanse our altars, to re-consecrate time, thought, and affection. It reminds us that God delights to restore what defilement seemed to steal.

The *menorah* also rebukes resignation. Many lament the darkness of our age. Moral confusion, spiritual apathy, and cultural hostility are the product of spiritual darkness. Yet *Hanukkah* insists that a single uncompromised flame can still transform a generation. "Arise, shine, for your light has come! The glory of *Adonai* has risen on you. For behold, darkness covers the earth, and deep darkness the peoples; but *Adonai* will arise upon you, and His glory will appear over you." (Isaiah 60:1–2) When we light candles of faith, prayer, and justice, we participate again in Judah Maccabee's legacy. We wage our own war for the holy places of our hearts, our communities, and our world.

Epilogue: The Hammer Echoes Still

History moves on and Rome will soon overshadow the weakened Hasmoneans. The Temple will rise higher under Herod before falling again. Yet *Hanukkah* endures. It whispers through centuries that reclaimed holiness can outlive destroyed kingdoms.

The hammer that struck idols in *Modiin* rings still in every act of faithful courage. Each refusal to bow to lesser deities and each endeavor to rebuild worship amidst ruins demonstrate the courage required to uphold the covenant. Its sound assures us that the covenant stands, that the light still burns, and that every generation can write its own verse in the long song of dedication.

May we, too, become modern Maccabees. Hammers of hope forged in prayer, wielded by compassion, striking not men but darkness until every altar glows again with the pure flame of *Adonai*. "The spirit of man is the lamp of *Adonai*, searching all his inmost being." (Proverbs 20:27) Let that inner lamp keep burning. The war for the Holy Place is never only history. Rather, it is happening wherever faith battles forgetfulness and wherever light insists on shining.

6

Kings and Priests
The Hasmonean Experiment

The smoke of rededication had scarcely cleared from the Temple courts when questions of governance began to stir. The House *of Hasmon* who were descendants of the priest Mattathias now led not merely warriors but a nation. Judah Maccabee's victories had preserved *Torah*, but leadership demanded more than courage. Should priests become princes? Could those who guarded worship also wield political authority?

In ancient Israel, priest and king were distinct offices.[41] Priests descended from Aaron, transmitting holiness while kings came from David's line, administering justice. The separation protected spiritual integrity. But now the throne of David lay vacant, prophecy silent, and the people longed for stability. Thus, out of necessity and divine mystery the priestly family assumed both mantles. What began as survival would soon turn into a dynasty.

---

[41] In Israel's Scriptures, kings and priests are distinct because God assigns their authority to different tribes and roles. The king is promised to David's line from Judah, while priesthood is given to Aaron's line within Levi, preventing their routine combination in one person (Genesis 49:10; Numbers 3:10; 2 Samuel 7:12–16). This separation is reinforced narratively: when Saul and later Uzziah intrude into priestly functions, they are judged, underscoring that sacrificial and cultic ministry belongs to the priests, while governance and military leadership belong to the king (1 Samuel 13:8–14; 2 Chronicles 26:16–21).

Simon the Hasmonean: A Priest on a Throne

After Judah's death in battle (160 BCE) and his brother Jonathan's execution years later, Simon emerged as leader. By 142 BCE Judah's homeland was weary of endless war. Simon negotiated with the Seleucid king Demetrius II, who granted substantial independence, remission of taxes, freedom of borders, and formal recognition of Jewish law. The people, reveling in hope, proclaimed Simon not only high priest but "ethnarch and commander of the Jews forever until a trustworthy prophet shall arise." (1 Maccabees 14:41)

This statement is astonishing because it reveals a community conscious that their experiment was provisional. Although they craved prophetic confirmation, none came. The spirit of prophecy had been quiet since Malachi. His last words of Scripture still echoed, "Behold, I am sending you Elijah the prophet before the coming of the great and terrible day of *Adonai*." (Malachi 3:23).

Simon ruled wisely. He fortified Jerusalem, expanded education, strengthened the Temple, and organized coinage inscribed with ancient symbols rather than pagan images. For once, Judea experienced both autonomy and peace.

The historian Josephus observed that under Simon, "Every man sat under his own vine and fig tree."[42] Words lifted from Zechariah's prophecy seemed alive again. But the seeds of contradiction sprouted quickly. Priestly

---

[42] 1 Maccabees 14:41; Flavius Josephus, H. St. J. Thackeray, 7:420–423.

sanctity had become political authority, and zeal for purity began to taste the power of position.

The Birth of the Hasmonean Dynasty

When Simon was assassinated by political rivals (134 BCE), his son John Hyrcanus succeeded him. Hyrcanus inherited not a revolution's fervor but rival factions, foreign conspiracies, and the temptations of prosperity.

He consolidated territory east of the Jordan and even destroyed the Samaritan temple on Mount Gerizim. His military expansion recalled David's conquests, but with it came the first coercive conversions of the *Idumeans* (Edomites). These conversions required the *Idumeans* to accept circumcision and live under *Torah* law to remain in the land. Political stability had birthed religious compulsion which is the dark shadow of zeal.[43]

Externally, Hyrcanus admired Greek culture. He built fortresses and palaces resembling Hellenistic designs, issued coins with Greek inscriptions, and indulged luxuries his father would have scorned. The earlier harmony between *Torah* and independence began to waver.

Upon Hyrcanus's death, civil strife erupted among his sons. The throne alternated between Aristobulus I and Alexander Jannaeus, both of whom took the title "king," a title the *Torah* never granted to priests. The Hasmonean

---

[43] Bourgel, Jonathan. "The Destruction of the Samaritan Temple by John Hyrcanus." Journal of Biblical Literature 135, no. 3 (2016): 505–523.

experiment had crossed from temporary guardianship into dynastic ambition.[44]

Aristobulus was the first to crown himself king and reigned only one year (104/103 BCE) yet set a precedent. In his brief rule he executed one brother and imprisoned his mother, revealing how swiftly zeal for God can warp into thirst for control. Scripture's ancient warning thus returned fulfilled, "It is not by power that a man prevails." (1 Samuel 2:9)

His brother Alexander Jannaeus (103–76 BCE) expanded territory further. The Galilee, Perea, and coastal cities fell to his army. He combined high-priestly garments with a soldier's sword, embodying simultaneous sanctity and severity.

He also provoked domestic crisis. Faithful Jews accused him of Sabbath violations and arrogance during *Sukkot*. When worshipers pelted him with citrons (*lulav* fruit) in protest, he retaliated brutally slaughtering thousands in the Temple precinct. The gulf between ruler and worshiper widened into trauma. During his reign two known camps within Judaism crystallized:

1. The Pharisees, who were champions of *Torah* fidelity, oral tradition, and ethical piety.

2. The Sadducees, who were priestly aristocrats aligned with Hellenistic influence and temple authority.

---

[44] Levine, Lee I. "The Age of Hellenism: Alexander the Great and the Rise and Fall of the Hasmonean Kingdom." In Jerusalem: Its Sanctity and Centrality to Judaism, Christianity, and Islam, edited by Lee I. Levine, 134–160. New York: Continuum, 1999.

Alexander sided with the Sadducees. Civil war raged within what had once been a covenant family. The land of dedication now bled under its own kings. When Alexander died, he counseled his queen, Salome Alexandra, to reconcile with the Pharisees. She reigned nine years in relative peace (76–67 BCE), restoring *Torah* scholarship and earning genuine affection. For a moment, righteousness and rule seemed to balance. Yet beneath perceived stability ambition waited.

The next generation rekindled strife. Salome's sons, Hyracnus II and Aristobulus II, quarreled violently over the throne. As a result, both appealed for arbitration to Rome, a rising power in the Mediterranean region. This fateful invitation would change the Jewish world forever. In 63 BCE the Roman general Pompey intervened, entered Jerusalem, and, violating the Holy of Holies, claimed control. Thus ended a century of independence gained by the Maccabees. The hammer that once shattered idols had fractured under pride. Foreign troops once again occupied the city. [45]

In hindsight, the national joy of Hanukkah transformed into a lament, as it became evident that freedom without humility had led back to servitude. "When pride comes, then comes disgrace, but with the humble is wisdom." (Proverbs 11:2)

---

[45] Josephus, Flavius. H. St. J. Thackeray, Books 13–14 (esp. 13.301–432; 14.1–79).

Spiritual Movements of a Fragmented Age

Although politics decayed, the period birthed extraordinary spiritual diversity. Much of the Judaism known to *Yeshua*'s generation took shape amid Hasmonean upheaval. Again, three movements previously created from chaos and confusion, not solidified during this era. The Pharisees who emphasized holiness for all, the Sadducees who were the guardians of privilege, and the Essenes who removed themselves from society for the sake of purity.

Moving beyond Temple ritual, the Pharisees taught holiness for all. They contended that purity laws extended beyond priests to encompass every household. Their study houses (synagogues) multiplied across villages. The pharisees codified prayers, blessings, and the ethical applications of *Torah*. Their creed echoed Micah 6:8, "He has told you, O man, what is good, and what *Adonai* is seeking from you—to practice justice, to love mercy, and to walk humbly with your God." Through their devotion, ordinary Jews learned that holiness belonged not to hierarchy but to heart.

The Sadducees, meanwhile, guarded Temple prerogative and rejected oral traditions. They emphasized written *Torah* alone, denied resurrection, and collaborated with whoever held political power. They maintained pageantry but lost prophetic pulse.

Disgusted by corruption, another group fled to the wilderness near the Dead Sea. Known later as the Essenes, they lived communally, awaited final deliverance, and copied Scriptures in purity. These copies give us, in modern times, the Dead Sea Scrolls. Their writings speak of two Messiahs, a priestly and a royal, reflecting longing for balance lost by the Hasmoneans.

Together these movements testify that even in turmoil, Israel's spiritual creativity did not die. When earthly crowns faltered, the hope of heaven grew stronger.[46]

Though Pompey placed Judea under nominal self-rule, real power shifted to Rome. Hyrcanus II remained High Priest. Yet his Idumean advisor Antipater who was the father of Herod maneuvered behind the scenes with Roman favor. Herod's ascent would later dwarf the Hasmoneans in architectural grandeur but would never match their faith. The Hasmonean experiment thus ended as monarchy without prophecy, priesthood without purity, and independence without integrity.[47] Yet God, who had promised David and enduring house, was already working behind the political curtains as silence prepared for a voice crying in the wilderness. A succession of failed kings had fueled the Jewish yearning for a righteous ruler.

Re-evaluating the Experiment

To study the Hasmoneans is to trace the paradox of pious success of how victory can undermine virtue. Their legacy instructs every generation of believers who wield influence.

---

[46] Flavius Josephus, *The Jewish War*, trans. G. A. Williamson (London: Penguin Classics, 1981), 131–140; Shaye J. D. Cohen, *From the Maccabees to the Mishnah*, 3rd ed. (Louisville: Westminster John Knox, 2014), 140–155.

[47] Josephus, Flavius. Jewish Antiquities. H. St. J. Thackeray, 14.1–18, 14.36–79.

- Lesson 1: Zeal Must Serve, Not Rule. The Maccabean fathers fought for *Torah*'s freedom. However, their sons used *Torah* for control. When good causes become identities instead of instruments, zeal blinds. Recall Paul's reflection centuries later, "I testify about them that they have zeal for God but not based on knowledge." (Romans 10:2)
- Lesson 2: Purity Without Humility Becomes Pride. Alexander Jannaeus enforced holiness by the sword. *Yeshua* would later offer it by the Spirit. The true sanctuary can never be coerced. Rather, it must be convinced.
- Lesson 3: Every Reform Needs Renewal. No revival stays pure automatically. As the *menorah's* oil needed daily replenishment, movements need continual repentance. History repeats because holiness requires maintenance.

Scholars label these years "intertestamental," but heaven was hardly silent. The voice of prophecy, though not preserved in canonical form, resonated in the hearts of sages and psalmists.

Texts like 1 Enoch, Testament of the Twelve Patriarchs, and Jubilees envisioned angelic warfare and future judgment. These prove that Israel's imagination still burned with expectation. Every failed ruler intensified hope for divine intervention. The term Messiah, once a ritual designation for anointed kings and priests, grew into the apocalyptic expectation of one sent from heaven to restore all things. The experiment of priestly monarchy thus trained the nation to long for One who could unite holiness and kingship legitimately. This priest-king will be fulfilled in the Son of David who is also the great High Priest.

The dual role attempted by the Hasmoneans foreshadows a pattern that Scripture completes in Messiah. In the Psalms David sang, "*Adonai* has sworn and will not relent: 'You are a kohen forever according to the order of Melchizedek.'" (Psalm 110:4)

Melchizedek, the king of Salem and priest of *El Elyon*, was the only figure to hold both offices in righteousness. The Hasmoneans reached for that ideal but without revelation's warrant. Their failure revealed humanity's inability to blend power and purity without divine mediation.

In *Yeshua*, prophecy declares the reality they sought. "He will sit and rule on His throne. Thus, He will be a *kohen* on His throne, and the counsel of peace will be between them both." (Zechariah 6:13) The Hasmonean throne crumbled while the heavenly priest-king endures.

As the century turned, Judea under Roman oversight grew restless. Pilgrims still streamed to the Second Temple, but prayers now included pleas for deliverance from foreign yoke. Every Passover psalm carried the double meaning of thanksgiving for Egypt's release and yearning for Rome's end.

Prophecy's silence sharpened expectation. Many recalled Balaam's oracle, "A star will come out of Jacob; a scepter will rise out of Israel." (Numbers 24:17) Speculative leaders claimed fulfillment while revolts flickered and failed. Among scholars, debates over resurrection and angels multiplied. Among peasants, stories of Elijah's return circulated. Among zealots, swords were hidden beneath cloaks.[48]

Through all of it, God shaped the stage for an arrival of a child-King born not to Hasmonean splendor, but to a humble northern village uniting again priestly compassion with royal authority.

The Hasmonean Legacy in Perspective

Historically, their dynasty accomplished far more than its moral lapses admit:

- **National Identity Preserved.** Without the Maccabean revolt, Judaism might have vanished in assimilation.
- **Language and Law Revived.** Hebrew that was nearly lost, survived and the *Torah* became daily norm.
- **Institutional Foundations.** The Sanhedrin evolved from Hasmonean councils, enabling continuity under later rule.

Yet spiritually, their experiment served as a cautionary parable that independence cannot substitute for intimacy with God. True kingship awaits a heart like David's and a priesthood like Melchizedek's.

Pharisees preserved their memory as heroes, but later rabbis judged their arrogance severely. Both views share truth. The Hasmoneans were instruments of deliverance

---

[48] Collins, John J. *The Scepter and the Star* (Grand Rapids: Eerdmans, 2010), 74–90, 120–135; John J. Collins, *The Apocalyptic Imagination* (Grand Rapids: Eerdmans, 2016), 72–85.

and warnings against pride. They were hammers who built and cracked the same altar.

Modern Resonance: Faith and Power Today

Their story continues to speak to communities that gain influence after persecution. When faith moves from margins to center, the old dangers return:

- Identification with power rather than purpose.
- Use of holiness as control rather than compassion.
- Neglect of prophetic voices in favor of comfort.

The Hasmonean mirror asks uncomfortable questions. Have we traded spiritual authenticity for success? Do we still wait for the righteous ruler, or have we crowned our own ambitions? The lesson endures that if priests become kings without divine calling, then worship becomes politics. When priests refuse kingship out of humility, God exalts them to true authority.

Despite decay, the Hasmonean generation's original dream remains sacred. A vision where the people of God live free to honor the *Torah*, where justice flows from the Temple, and knowledge of God fills the land. That vision was not discarded, but rather, it was deferred until fulfilled perfectly in the Messiah's kingdom. "The scepter will not pass from Judah, nor the ruler's staff from between his feet, until He to whom it belongs will come." (Genesis 49:10)

The lineage of the Maccabees fades into history, but the promise woven through Judah's tribe endures. Whereas their dynasty ended under Rome's heel, *Yeshua*'s reign begins with a crown of thorns and ends in eternal glory.

Reflection: The Altar and the Throne

Standing on Mount Zion today, one can almost hear the echoes of the chants of priests, the clang of soldiers, and the debates of scribes. All these voices ask a single question, "Who rules this Holy Place?" The Hasmoneans answered, "We do." Alternatively, the prophets answered, "*Adonai* does." Their story invites every believer to examine personal realms of authority and the heart's parliament where devotion and ambition contend. Are we guardians of worship or governors of self-interest? The experiment continues within us each day.

Hanukkah's lamps testified that dedication belongs to God alone. The Hasmoneans forgot that truth while Messiah restores it. His kingdom possesses the power they craved and the purity they lost. When during worship we pray, "May Your kingdom come," we invoke the completion of all failed experiments, and the complete reunion of holiness and governance under perfect love.

Until that day arrives, the calling remains the same as in Simon's proclamation to serve faithfully "until a trustworthy prophet shall arise." (1 Maccabees 14:41) That Prophet has come, yet His voice still calls us from heaven, "Repent, for the kingdom of heaven is at hand." (Matthew 4:17)

Epilogue – History's Teacher

The Hasmonean century bridges the courage of the Maccabees and the birth of Messiah. It teaches that revival without humility decays, that freedom without righteousness enslaves, and that political success without spiritual surrender topples faster than tyranny.

Yet it also reminds us that heaven wastes no history. Every triumph and failure became texture in God's larger narrative of *Torah* defended, faith refined, and expectation heightened. Through flawed kings and faithful remnant alike, the divine promise marched forward. "For His dominion is an everlasting dominion that will never pass away—and His kingdom is one that will not be destroyed." (Daniel 7:14)

The Hasmonean halls crumble, but that kingdom endures. Their experiment, though marred, prepared humanity to recognize true kingship when it appeared wrapped in humility, riding on a donkey, and whispering forgiveness from a cross.

Thus, the story closes not in despair but in gratitude. For even in failure, the God of Israel writes covenant lessons that outshine every crown.

Part III: Rome, Revival, and Revelation

7

Herod's Kingdom
The Great Builder
and His Temple

In 63 BCE the clatter of Roman spears echoed through Jerusalem's gates. General Pompey the Great surveyed the city, breached its walls, and entered the Holy of Holies which was the most forbidden place on earth to outsiders. His curiosity cost Israel its remaining sovereignty.

Rome, the new master of the Mediterranean, declared Judea a client kingdom under imperial authority. For more than a century after the Maccabees' victories, Jewish independence had flickered. But now, the lamp dimmed.[49] Yet even amid subjugation, *Adonai* was weaving history's tapestry toward redemption. The precision of His providence would soon align prophets, politics, and a carpenter's cradle.

Enter Herod: An Idumean Prince in a Jewish World

Among those who welcomed Rome was Antipater, an Idumean whose family had accepted circumcision under

---

[49] Sharon, Nadav. 2019. "The Roman Conquest of Judaea (63 BCE)." In The Roman Province of Judea: A Historical Overview. Provo, UT: BYU Studies. Accessed April 5, 2026. https://byustudies.byu.edu/article/the-roman-province-of-judea-a-historical-overview.

the Hasmoneans. He served as advisor to Hyrcanus II and was considered a Master of Diplomacy with Rome. His son Herod, born around 73 BCE, inherited both political cunning and ambition that knew no moral restraint.

Educated in both Jewish tradition and Greco-Roman culture, Herod possessed the rare combination of provincial knowledge and imperial instinct. He cultivated friendships with powerful Romans, including Mark Antony and later Caesar Augustus, who would crown him "King of the Jews" in 37 BCE.[50]

It was a tragic irony that a man who wasn't fully Jewish was ruling a people who yearned for David's heir. Rome found in him a loyal client capable of both intimidation and intrigue. Judea would know peace, but it would be the uneasy peace of a sheathed sword but ever visible.

Herod's early reign was soaked in blood. He eliminated every potential rival. In his exterminations, he executed the former Hasmonean prince Antigonus (ordered by Antony), his brother-in-law Aristobulus (drowned to appease the jealous court), and eventually his beloved but politically inconvenient wife, Mariamne. He also murdered three of his sons on charges of treason.[51]

Emperor Augustus reportedly remarked, "Better to be Herod's pig than his son." [52] Ironically, the joke acknowledged Herod's adherence to Jewish dietary restrictions against pork, even as he violated every moral

---

[50] Cohen, Shaye J. D. From the Maccabees to the *Mishnah*, 3rd ed. (Louisville: Westminster John Knox Press, 2014), 38–44.
[51] Richardson, Peter. Herod: King of the Jews and Friend of the Romans (Columbia, SC: University of South Carolina Press, 1996), 135–152.
[52] Macrobius. Saturnalia. 2.4.11.

principle of the *Torah*. Fear, not legitimacy, secured his throne.

Yet Herod understood that monuments outlive memory within human imagination. If he could build enough glory, perhaps posterity would forget the screams in his palace halls. Thus began one of the greatest building campaigns of the ancient world.

Herod's works stretched from Masada, the desert citadel overlooking the Dead Sea, to Herodium, an artificial mountain he fashioned as his own tomb. He rebuilt the harbor of Caesarea Maritima, dedicating it to Caesar and crowning it with a temple to Rome's genius. Aqueducts, theaters, and palaces dotted the landscape. However, all these projects served to remake Judea in the image of the empire and himself in the role of the deliverer. Thus, he placed his attention on Jerusalem, the navel of the world.[53]

The Vision of a New Temple

The Second Temple, rebuilt under Zerubbabel centuries earlier, still functioned but looked modest beside the marble temples of Athens and Rome. Herod proposed to rebuild it entirely, both as political masterpiece and as gesture of piety to win Jewish loyalty.

Many priests hesitated with memories of foreign desecration still fresh in their minds. But Herod promised to finance the enterprise lavishly and to maintain ritual

---

[53] Netzer, Ehud. *The Architecture of Herod, the Great Builder* (Tübingen: Mohr Siebeck, 2006), 3–35.

purity. To prevent suspicion, he trained 1,000 priests in masonry so only sanctified hands would touch holy stones.

Construction began about 20 BCE and continued, in stages, until just before the Roman destruction in 70 CE. The historian Josephus wrote that the project employed ten thousand skilled workers and gleamed like snow in sunlight.

The Temple complex occupied nearly 35 acres. It was twice the area of modern Jerusalem's Old City quarter where its retaining walls still stand.[54] Its grandeur was so breath-taking that later rabbis declared, "He who has not seen Herod's Temple has never seen a beautiful building in his life."[55] Herod's Temple was not just engineering. It was a theological narrative cast in stone.

- White limestone walls reflected brilliant light, symbolizing purity.
- Gold-plated ornamentation shimmered like dawn, recalling Psalm 29's "beauty of holiness."
- Colonnaded courts separated Gentile, women, Israelites, and priests, dramatizing layered holiness yet inviting the nations to gaze in wonder.
- The Holy Place and Most Holy Place followed Mosaic design. Yet the absence of the ark of the covenant, lost since Babylon, was a silent reminder that divine presence awaited restoration.

---

[54] Satterthwaite, Philip E. "The Temple of Herod." In New Testament History, Culture, and Society: A Background to the Texts of the New Testament, edited by Lincoln H. Blumell, 141–160. Provo, UT: Religious Studies Center, Brigham Young University, 2019.
[55] Bava Batra 4a.

To many, Herod's Temple appeared as fulfillment of Haggai 2:9, "The latter glory of this House will be greater than the former." Its physical splendor eclipsed Solomon's, yet spiritual glory had not yet returned. The radiance of the *Shekhinah* had not descended. The stage was built, but heaven's light had yet to enter.

The Socio-Political Landscape

Herod's construction boom created employment and infrastructure but deepened inequality. Heavy taxation funded marble, not mercy. While cities dazzled, peasants starved. The gap between priestly elite and agrarian poor widened further.

To manage unrest, Herod appointed his own high priests, dismissing lineal claimants. The office once reserved for Aaron's descendants became political currency. By manipulating the Temple hierarchy, he controlled not only governance but the religious imagination itself. This manipulation birthed cynicism among commoners and fostered the sectarian landscape described in earlier chapters. Pharisees taught holiness through study, Sadducees entrenched deeper within Temple wealth, and Essenes retreating to purity enclaves.[56]

Many came to regard the Temple, ironically, as both the sign of national restoration and a symbol of oppression.

---

[56] Carter, Warren. Matthew and the Margins: A Sociopolitical and Religious Reading. Maryknoll, NY: Orbis Books, 2000, 23–31.

With that backdrop, prophetic hope intensified that God would send a true son of David to restore righteousness.[57]

Beneath Herod's marble surface, faith endured quietly. The synagogue movement thrived as rabbis in Galilee and Judea cultivated *Torah* study accessible to all. While incense smoked before Herod's gilded veil, villages still read Deuteronomy to children each Sabbath. Pilgrims ascended for feasts singing Psalms 120–134. "I was glad when they said to me, 'Let us go up to the House of *Adonai.*'" (Psalm 122:1) In their ascent songs hope found harmony. Even a compromised temple remained a meeting point with heaven.

Herod's courts filled with different languages. Latin soldiers, Greek merchants, Aramaic preachers each added threads to the tapestry of providence. The empire unwittingly created roads, ports, and lingua franca that would later carry the gospel. God once again used Rome, as He had used Persia and Babylon, to prepare His messengers' highway.

The closer Herod came to mortality, the more paranoia gripped him. Ailing with disease, he executed anyone suspected of disloyalty including his two favorite sons, Alexander and Aristobulus. According to Josephus, he even ordered prominent Jewish leaders to be killed at his death so that mourning would fill the land. Fortunately, that command was ignored.[58]

---

[57] Wright, N. T. Jesus and the Victory of God. Christian Origins and the Question of God, Vol. 2. Minneapolis: Fortress Press, 1996, 332–340.

[58] Josephus, Flavius. Antiquities of the Jews. Book 16, §§392–394; Book 17, §§173–189

Physically decrepit, spiritually empty, the "Great" lay dying in Jericho. Not far north, in the obscure village of Bethlehem, a child was born whose lineage stretched back to David. The Gospel remembers the collision of these two kingdoms, "After *Yeshua* was born in Bethlehem of Judea in the days of King Herod, *magi* from the east came to Jerusalem." (Matthew 2:1)

Herod heard whispers of another "King of the Jews." Consumed by jealousy, he decreed slaughter on Bethlehem's infants. The tyrant who had rebuilt the Temple now stained Judea with innocent blood once more.[59]

Shortly after, Herod died (4 BCE). His empire fractured among his sons, Archelaus, Antipas, and Philip, each ruling a divided province under Roman supervision. The dream of autonomous monarchy collapsed completely. Yet divine purpose advanced in Bethlehem's swaddled Prince.

Herod's Temple in *Yeshua*'s World

By the time *Yeshua* began teaching, Herod's Temple dominated Jerusalem's skyline. Every pilgrim who entered the city passed through its vast courts while its rituals framed daily life.

- The Court of Gentiles hosted money-changers exchanging foreign currency for temple shekels, an economy masquerading as piety. When *Yeshua*

---

[59] Fruchtenbaum, Arnold G. The Footsteps of the Messiah: A Study of the Sequence of Prophetic Events. 2nd rev. ed. San Antonio, TX: Ariel Ministries, 2003, 221–226.

overturned their tables (Matthew 21:12), He struck at systemic exploitation, not commerce itself.

- The Royal Stoa, a colonnade along the southern wall, served as meeting hall and marketplace. Here merchants mingled with scholars debating *Torah*.
- Solomon's Colonnade, on the eastern side, provided shade for teachers and disciples. This later became a meeting place for the early believers after the resurrection (Acts 3:11).

The Temple was paradox of fulfillment and foreshadowing. It was both a house of prayer and den of injustice. When *Yeshua* predicted its destruction, "Not one stone will be left upon another." (Mark 13:2) His prophecy sounded impossible since the walls seemed indestructible. Yet forty years later Rome would prove Him right.

Theology of the Magnificent Structure

Herod's Temple challenges every generation's understanding of worship. Its beauty reminds us that aesthetics can magnify awe, but also that splendor can camouflage hypocrisy. *Adonai* allowed its splendor because He would soon replace stone with Spirit. The prophet Isaiah had already announced, "The heavens are My throne, and the earth is My footstool. Where then is the House, you would build for Me?" (Isaiah 66:1)

Herod's marble could not contain heaven. The real temple, the Messiah Himself, was walking among them. As *Yeshua* declared, "Destroy this temple, and in three days I will raise it up." (John 2:19) Only after resurrection would His disciples understand that He spoke of His body. The dwelling of God with humanity had shifted from architecture to incarnation.

Herod's death left Judea restless. Within a few decades, Roman procurators such as Pontius Pilate would govern directly, inflaming tensions that culminated in the Jewish revolt of 66–70 CE. Herod's urbanization profoundly impacted Jewish life in several areas. Caesarea Maritima provided a gateway for commerce and for later missionary journeys of Paul. Masada's fortress would become the rebels' last stand, providing a tragic epilogue to national resistance. Herod's Temple platform expanded beyond Zerubbabel's original footprint and remains the foundation of today's Western Wall, a focal point of Jewish prayer. Thus, paradoxically, a tyrant's vanity project became both Israel's national symbol and enduring spiritual landmark.[60]

Herod illustrates the tragic blend of piety and pride that haunts every age. He built the most magnificent house for God yet could not open the smallest chamber of his own heart to Him. His life warns leaders in every generation that influence, ideology, and infrastructure cannot substitute for intimacy with *Adonai*. True kings build altars, not monuments to self. *Yeshua*'s contrasting model, a humble carpenter rather than marble monarch, reveals heaven's valuation of power. "For everyone who exalts himself will be humbled, and the one who humbles himself will be exalted." (Luke 14:11) Herod exalted himself in stone, but God exalted His Son in resurrection.

---

[60] Bauckham, Richard. The Bible in the Contemporary World: Hermeneutical Ventures. Grand Rapids: Eerdmans, 2015, 67–82.

Jerusalem as World Crossroad

By the first century CE, Jerusalem's population may have reached several hundred thousand during pilgrimage festivals. Herod's infrastructure of mosaic-paved streets, aqueducts, and massive gates made these gatherings possible.[61]

Romans saw the city as provincial capital, the Greeks viewed it with philosophical curiosity, and the Jews embraced it as the center of their covenant. Into that convergence of cultures stepped *Yeshua*, teaching that the kingdom of God was not coming with visible architecture but was already "within you." His words redefined sacred geography.

After His ascension, early believers continued attending Temple prayers (Acts 2:46) while proclaiming that the new covenant promise of Jeremiah 31:31 had begun. The physical Temple still stood, but the spiritual reality it foreshadowed was being fulfilled.

In 66 CE open revolt exploded. Rome responded with overwhelming might. Four years later armies under Titus annihilated Jerusalem and burned the Temple. Josephus describes a horrifying scene of apocalyptic sorrow, where flame-reflected gold melts down marble steps.[62]

Herod's masterpiece, still undergoing renovations, became rubble. Only a few stones that formed the retaining wall survived. These stones were so large that later

---

[61] Magness, Jodi. "Journey to Jerusalem: Pilgrims and Immigrants in the Time of Herod." Biblical Archaeology Review 48, no. 4 (Fall 2022).
[62] Josephus, Flavius. The Jewish War. 6.249–271.

pilgrims referred to them as "the last witnesses." To this day Jews pray before them, touching not Herod's glory but the persistence of hope. Thus ended the material symbol of God's dwelling, but not His covenant presence. As *Yeshua* had told the Samaritan woman, "The hour is coming when you will worship the Father neither on this mountain nor in Jerusalem . . . but in spirit and truth." (John 4:21-23) The destruction that Herod's hubris made inevitable cleared spiritual space for that universal worship.

Modern Echoes: Faith and Architecture

Herod's building compels reflection on the relationship between faith and beauty. Architecture can testify to divine majesty, yet when divorced from righteousness it rots into idolatry. Every generation constructs its "temples" (cathedrals, institutions, ministries, etc.) and must ponder whether these structures glorify God or itself. The lesson of Herod's Temple is not aesthetic minimalism but moral alignment. Excellence honors God only when the builder's heart bows before Him. When believers create art, music, or scholarship from devotion rather than ego, they redeem what Herod perverted. Magnificence motivated by worship, not self-promotion, honors *Adonai*.

When *Yeshua* entered the courts overturning tables, He quoted Isaiah 56:7, "My House will be called a House of Prayer for all nations." That prophetic claim contrasted sharply with Herod's exclusionary design. The "Court of the Gentiles" meant as witness space, had become a money-market. In restoring prayer, *Yeshua* restored the Temple's universal mission.

His body hung on Golgotha within sight of Herod's white walls. When He breathed His last, "the curtain of the Temple was torn in two from top to bottom." (Matthew 27:51) Heaven itself declared that access was now open. No marble veil could contain divine mercy. The world's true sanctuary hung not with gold but with flesh redeemed.

Herod built upward while Messiah builds inward. One sought immortality through monuments as the other through transformed hearts. To serve God today is to choose the carpenter's blueprint over the king's structure. We build hospitals, schools, and sanctuaries, but their holiness depends on humility, justice, and love. Whenever faith trades character for audacity, Herod's ghost returns.

Yet even through Herod, God kept His promise. His Temple platform provided the very stage for *Yeshua*'s ministry, His trials, and His early followers' witness. Thus, divine providence redeemed human pride. As Joseph long ago said, "You meant evil against me, but God meant it for good." (Genesis 50:20)

Epilogue: From Marble to Messiah

When travelers today walk the Western Wall's stones or view Temple Mount's remnants, they touch a paradox. The enigma of beauty born of tyranny and sanctity surviving desecration. The stones cannot speak, yet if they could, they would echo *Yeshua*'s promise, "I tell you, if these keep silent, the stones will cry out." (Luke 19:40)

Herod's grandeur has faded into dust, but the one who preached in its courts still reigns. He is the true "builder of the House" foretold in Zechariah 6:12–13, "Behold, a man whose Name is Branch! He will branch out from his place and build the Temple of *Adonai* . . . He will bear glory and sit and rule on His throne."

What Herod attempted in stone, Messiah accomplishes in spirit. The promise continues beyond ruin, and every believer, reconciled by the Lamb, becomes a living stone in a temple not made by hands. "You also, as living stones, are being built up as a spiritual house." (1 Peter 2:5) So ends Herod's chapter and begins ours. We are a kingdom of humility, not marble; of mercy, not monuments; and of a King who serves and a Temple that lives forever.

8

Many Voices, One Hope
The Movements of the Time

By the first century BCE, Herod's marble courtyards gleamed and pilgrims once again filled Jerusalem at every feast. Yet beneath the hymns and incense lay growing fracture. Within one small land, four great currents of thought flowed. Each claiming to represent the true Israel.

Foreign armies had come and gone, prophets had fallen silent, and empires now dictated taxation, trade, and peace. Still, the covenant people refused to vanish. They argued, prayed, and rebelled in the conviction that God had not abandoned them. Even if His presence seemed hidden behind Roman banners.

The diversity of this period was not confusion but life under pressure. Faith was being forged anew. Out of it would emerge both rabbinic Judaism and the Messianic movement that would ripple into every culture on earth.

The Pharisees – Holiness in Every House

The *Perushim* (Pharisees), meaning "Separated Ones," began as a lay reform movement during the Hasmonean chaos. Their goal was not separation from community but from corruption. If priests had compromised and kings had tyrannized, ordinary Israelites would live as if each table were an altar and each home a miniature sanctuary. The Pharisees emphasized:

- *Torah* plus Tradition. The Pharisees revered the written *Torah* yet believed that an oral interpretation had been given to Moses on Sinai. This "oral *Torah*" guided application in daily contexts. The written law gave commandments, but the oral law gave instruction about how to observe *Shabbat*, purity laws, or tithes in common life. Centuries later, these traditions would be codified in the Mishnah.[63]

- Holiness for All. They taught that ceremonial purity was not limited to priests in the Temple. A farmer eating bread in Galilee should treat his meal with the same reverence as a priest eating showbread. Religion left the Sanctuary and entered the kitchen.

- Resurrection and Afterlife. The Pharisees affirmed resurrection and angels, drawing upon Daniel's vision, "Many of those who sleep in the dust of the earth will awake—some to everlasting life and others to everlasting shame." (Daniel 12:2) They

---

[63] The *Mishnah* is a foundational collection of Jewish oral laws and teachings, compiled and redacted in the late 2nd to early 3rd century CE under the leadership of Rabbi Judah ha-Nasi. It is the earliest major written form of the Oral *Torah*, preserving legal traditions and interpretations that had previously been transmitted by repetition and memorization. The work is organized into six thematic "orders" (*Zeraim, Moed, Nashim, Nezikin, Kodashim, Tohorot*), which together contain 63 tractates addressing topics such as agriculture, festivals, family law, civil and criminal law, sacrifices, and ritual purity. The *Mishnah* does not follow the biblical narrative sequence but arranges material by subject, offering concise rulings and often preserving multiple rabbinic opinions side by side. It became the core text studied and expanded by later rabbis in the *Gemara*, and together *Mishnah* and *Gemara* form the *Talmud*, the central text of rabbinic Judaism.

saw history moving toward a climactic day of judgment when the righteous would be vindicated.

- Providence and Human Freedom. God ruled all things but granted humans moral choice. This delicate dance between sovereignty and ethics became central to later theology.[64]

Because the Pharisees emphasized teaching rather than sacrifice, they gained immense respect among the people. Their scribes established local synagogues, saturating daily life with study. They were not monks or politicians. Rather, they were interpreters. No wonder *Yeshua* often debated them. They spoke the same language of righteousness and repentance. His sharpest words were for hypocrisy, not for devotion itself. He even affirmed their teaching when lived sincerely, "The *Torah* scholars and Pharisees sit on the seat of Moses. So, whatever they tell you, do and observe—but do not do what they do, for they say and do not do." (Matthew 23:2-3) From their dedication to Scripture, rabbinic Judaism would later flower after the Temple's fall. This provides proof that the Word, not walls, sustains a people.

The Sadducees – Guardians of the Status Quo

At the opposite end of the spectrum stood the *Tz'dukim*, likely deriving their name from Zadok, priest of Solomon's day. They were aristocrats who owned land and high priests who controlled Temple affairs. The Sadducees maintained a theology of literalism and limits:

---

[64] Sanders, E. P. Judaism: Practice and Belief, 63 BCE–66 CE. London: SCM Press, 1992, 272–310.

- Written *Torah* Only. They rejected oral tradition, insisting that only what was written was binding. Because resurrection and angels were less explicit in the Pentateuch, they denied them. Luke records them approaching *Yeshua* with skepticism about life after death. (Luke 20:27)
- Free Will Over Providence. They stressed human autonomy. To them, fate did not govern decisions.
- Focus on Ritual and Power. Their influence clung to the Temple treasury and Sanhedrin seats. They cooperated with Rome, viewing compromise as practical wisdom.[65]

The irony of the Sadducees is tragic. When the Temple fell in 70 CE, their world collapsed. With the collapse of the Temple, their theology could not survive without it. They vanished from history, leaving behind a warning that faith anchored only to institutions cannot outlive them.

The Essenes – Purity in Exile

While Pharisees reasoned in towns and Sadducees schemed in palaces, another community chose the wilderness. The Essenes, likely based at Qumran near the Dead Sea, withdrew entirely from what they deemed a corrupt priesthood.

Archaeology and Scrolls reveal an austere monastic society. Members took ritual baths daily, ate communal meals, and devoted themselves to copying Scripture. Their

---

[65] Grabbe, Lester L. Judaism from Cyrus to Hadrian. Vol. 2, The Roman Period. Minneapolis: Fortress Press, 1992, 410–422.

governing text, the Community Rule, called them the "Sons of Light," sworn to oppose the "Sons of Darkness."

They awaited a final war by which God would cleanse the earth. Unlike the Sadducees, they believed in angels and detailed eschatology. Unlike the Pharisees, they abandoned cities, seeking ultimate purity before the dawn.[66]

Their War Scroll portrays cosmic conflict between Belial, the prince of wickedness, versus the heavenly host. Yet even amid severity, their writings throb with hope, "Blessed be He who has kept truth for those who love Him, and the covenant of faith for those who cling to it." (1QH)[67]

Through them we glimpse Judaism's mystical side. They had a longing to see heaven's order mirrored on earth. Their preservation of Scripture ensured that, two millennia later, the Dead Sea Scrolls would confirm the astonishing fidelity of the biblical text.

The Zealots – Freedom at the Edge of the Sword

The fourth movement sprang not from scholars or monks but from patriots. The Zealots, or *Kanu'im*, believed violent uprising was the only faithful response to foreign rule. They traced inspiration to Phinehas, who once struck down blasphemy with a spear. Carrying daggers beneath cloaks (*Sicarii*), they targeted collaborators and Roman officials alike. Their creed was "No king but God."

---

[66] Vermes, Geza. The Complete Dead Sea Scrolls in English. Revised ed. London: Penguin Books, 2011, 67–115.
[67] Ibid., 160–190.

Among their heroes was Judas the Galilean, who in 6 CE led a revolt against the census tax, declaring that paying tribute to Caesar was treason against Heaven. His movement was crushed, but his cry echoed through the following decades until the revolt of 66 CE.[68]

Ironically, extreme zeal for God produced results opposite to their hopes. Their violence invited Roman retaliation, culminating in Jerusalem's destruction. Yet their passion also expressed an unquenchable thirst for deliverance. *Yeshua*, who felt the emotion he called "violence to the kingdom," redirected it toward peace. When one disciple drew a sword in Gethsemane, He answered, "Put your sword back into its place—for all who take up the sword shall perish by the sword." (Matthew 26:52)

Beyond Labels – The Ordinary Faithful

Not every Jew identified with a faction. The vast majority were humble villagers, farmers, fishermen, and artisans. These commoners simply kept *Torah*, attended synagogue, paid taxes, and prayed for Messiah. These *Am Ha'aretz*, "people of the land," bore the weight of imperial pressure yet sustained community life. Their devotion was practical. They sanctified meals through blessings, marked time through feasts, and sang psalms while sowing seed.

---

[68] Horsley, Richard A. Bandits, Prophets, and Messiahs: Popular Movements in the Time of Jesus. Harrisburg, PA: Trinity Press International, 1999, 33–52.

Yeshua spoke most often to the people of their world, not in palaces or academies, but on boats, in fields, and at marketplaces. Their simplicity provided fertile soil for the good news of the Kingdom. Centuries of prophecy had sown a vocabulary of redemption. Daniel's visions of heavenly man and everlasting kingdom mingled with Isaiah's Servant songs and Zechariah's oracles. By the first century, these threads wove intense expectation that deliverance was near.

The different groups imagined different fulfillments and through various Messianic ideals. The Pharisees waited for a Davidic ruler to restore *Torah* justice. The Essenes envisioned two Messiahs manifesting in a priestly one to purify worship and a royal one to conquer nations. The Zealots expected a warrior to deliver a crushed Rome. Many Apocalyptic teachers, channeling Daniel and Enoch, foresaw cosmic upheaval, angelic armies, and judgment.

This diversity did not signify unbelief but a shared conviction that history was charged with divine intervention. Even outside Judea, diasporic Jews spread hope through synagogues across the empire while Gentile "God-fearers" listened eagerly and were drawn to ethical monotheism and a vision of a coming age of peace.[69]

The Bible had become a living library shaping identity everywhere. The *Torah* anchored law, the Prophets promised renewal, and the Psalms voiced longing.

---

[69] Wright, N. T. The New Testament and the People of God. Christian Origins and the Question of God, Vol. 1. Minneapolis: Fortress Press, 1992, 280–338.

Translations into Greek (*Septuagint*) and Aramaic (*Targums*) allowed accessibility across regions. Psalm 2, read in light of oppression, inspired political and spiritual resistance. "Why do the nations rage, and the peoples plot a vain thing? . . . 'I have set My King upon Zion, My holy mountain.'" (Psalm 2:1, 6) Isaiah offered solace, "Then the eyes of the blind will be opened and the ears of the deaf unstopped. Then the lame will leap like a deer." (Isaiah 35:5-6)

Every festival retold these hopes. *Pesach* memorialized exodus, *Shavuot* remembered revelation, and *Sukkot* celebrated the joy of harvest. All feasts anticipating the kingdom to come. Even the practice of daily prayer embodied expectation. The *Amidah* petitioned, "Speedily cause the Branch of David, Your servant, to flourish."[70] Faith became rhythm, not theory.

Under oppression, imagination turned skyward. Apocalyptic visions interpreted world events as spiritual warfare. Books like 1 Enoch, Jubilees, and later 2 Baruch described angelic intermediaries, heavenly tablets, and divine judgment. They declared that God was not absent. Instead, He was unveiling His plan through symbolism accessible to the faithful.

---

[70] The *Amidah* is the central "standing" prayer of Jewish daily worship, recited three times a day and traditionally regarded as the core of the liturgy. Known also as the *Shemoneh Esrei* ("Eighteen"), it originally contained eighteen blessings, later expanded to nineteen, arranged in three sections: opening praises of God, a middle series of petitions for personal and communal needs, and closing blessings of thanksgiving and peace. The prayer is usually said while standing with feet together, facing Jerusalem, first silently by each worshiper and then, in traditional communities, repeated aloud by the prayer leader.

Though modern readers hear in these texts outlines of Revelation, for ancient Jews they were pastoral reassurance that chaos is controlled by heaven's timetable. Every empire was merely another beast soon to fall. This cosmic perspective produced resilience. Their hope transcended politics and it expected a new creation. The conviction that holiness now participates in a world yet to be revealed nurtured courage, non-conformity, and compassion.

The Rise of Schools and Teachers

In towns like *Tzippori*, *Beth She'an*, and Jerusalem, academies formed where scribes debated *halakhah* (law) and *aggadah* (exposition). Two primary schools emerged in the late first century BCE: Hillel and Shammai.

- Hillel, known for compassion and flexibility, summarized *Torah*, "What is hateful to you, do not do to your fellow. This is the whole *Torah*; the rest is commentary."[71]
- Shammai, a stricter and nationalistic teacher, emphasized separation from Gentiles and rigid adherence.

Their disputes prepared the framework for rabbinic decision-making involving dynamic, reasoned, discussions that were grounded in community discussion.[72] Into this world of argument and ethics stepped *Yeshua*, whose teachings often aligned with

---

[71] Babylonian *Talmud*, *Shabbat* 31a.
[72] Sanders, E. P. Judaism: Practice and Belief, 63 BCE–66 CE. London: SCM Press, 1992.

Hillel's mercy yet transcended both with divine authority in His sermon on the mount, "You have heard . . . but I tell you . . . "(Matthew 5)

Roman oppression and heavy taxation devastated rural families. Tenant farmers lost ancestral lands and fishermen paid tolls to use their own waters. Many lived one failed harvest away from ruin.

Into this desperation came itinerant preachers promising God's breakthrough. Some claimed to be prophets while others led followers into the wilderness expecting miracles. Josephus recounts multiple pseudo-messiahs in these decades, each swiftly crushed by Rome. Yet each failure intensified yearning.[73]

When John the Immerser appeared in the Jordan wilderness, clothed in camel hair and quoting Isaiah 40:3, "Prepare the way of *Adonai*," people flooded to him because the time finally felt right. They longed not for politics but for purity and pardon.

Though Jewish faith remained the anchor, Greek philosophy filled the air. In Alexandria, Jewish thinker Philo interpreted *Torah* through Platonic ideas, describing the Logos as divine reason and as the mediator between God and creation.

Elsewhere, Stoicism's call for virtue, Epicureanism's pursuit of tranquility, and Cynicism's radical simplicity interacted with Jewish ethics. When Paul later preached in Athens, he engaged that same intellectual climate. Second Temple Judaism, thus, was neither isolated nor

---

[73] Horsley, Richard A. Bandits, 29–52.

naïve. Rather, it was part of a global conversation about meaning.[74]

The Temple as Center and Symbol

Despite sectarian disputes, all movements oriented toward the Temple. Pilgrims from as far as Spain and Persia brought half-shekel offerings. Priests continued daily sacrifices, Levites sang psalms, and incense rose morning and evening. Josephus records that during festivals, over two million pilgrims might flow into Jerusalem. Though not literal census perhaps, but evidence of scale. The Temple was Israel's heartbeat, the axis where earth kissed heaven.[75]

Yet prophets' words haunted worshipers, "My House will be called a House of Prayer for all nations." (Isaiah 56:7) Some longed for inclusive holiness and others defended exclusivity. This debate over the question of "Who belongs?" would ignite when *Yeshua* welcomed tax collectors, sinners, Samaritans, and Gentiles into fellowship.

Though absent from official councils, women played crucial spiritual roles. They managed household observances of *Shabbat, kashrut,* and festival preparation. These daily tasks were crucial in preserving covenant identity. Pharisaic sources note righteous women known for charity and study. The school of Hillel advocated for a

---

74 Wright, N. T. Paul and the Faithfulness of God. Christian Origins and the Question of God, Vol. 4. Minneapolis: Fortress Press, 2013, 160–205.
75 Josephus, Flavius. The Jewish War. 6.422–427.

progressive approach, encouraging its students to teach their daughters *Torah*.[76] The echo of prophetic Scripture empowered them. Miriam the prophetess, Deborah the judge, Huldah the teacher, and later, Anna the prophetess would fast and pray in Herod's Temple awaiting redemption, proclaiming *Yeshua* when He arrived (Luke 2:36–38). Her story embodies the transition from expectation to fulfillment.

Despite divisions, most Jews shared unbreakable convictions:

1. Monotheism. *Adonai Echad!* (Hear O Israel, *Adonai* is One.)
2. Covenant Identity. Circumcision and Sabbath marked belonging.
3. Scriptural Authority. The *Torah* was divine revelation.
4. Ethical Responsibility. Justice and mercy are expressions of holiness.
5. Hope in Redemption. Belief that God would send deliverance.

These anchors kept Israel one people under many banners. They argued fiercely yet prayed the same psalms. As the *Talmud* later observed, "Disagreements for the sake of heaven will endure." Their diversity was not destruction but dialogue that prepared a world to recognize the voice of heaven when it spoke again. These

---

[76] Safrai, Shmuel. *The Jewish People in the First Century, Vol. 2: The Social Structure of the Jewish Community in Palestine in the Period of the Mishnah and Talmud*. Edited by S. Safrai and M. Stern. Assen: Van Gorcum, 1976.

various streams of thought provided a definite shape for the Messianic movement:

1. Vocabulary of the Kingdom. The Pharisees' teaching about the rule of Heaven supplied categories such as repentance, righteousness, and resurrection that *Yeshua* used. However, He universalized them.

2. Purity and Spirit. The Essenes' emphasis on immersion foreshadowed John's baptism of repentance.

3. Zeal Re-interpreted. Where Zealots sought freedom through violence, *Yeshua* taught deliverance through forgiveness.

4. Temple and Sacrifice. As Sadducean ritual decayed, His body became the new dwelling of divine presence.

Thus, every strand of Israel's religious landscape found correction and completion in Him. He was not an outsider but the culmination.

Rome and the Everyday Cross

Roman taxation pressed hardest on Galilee, breeding resentment and creativity alike. Herod Antipas' new capital, Tiberias, stood only a few miles from Capernaum. There *Yeshua* would later call disciples from nets filled with Roman-taxed fish. The daily burden of the Roman empire made His pronouncement, "Blessed are the poor in spirit, for theirs is the kingdom of heaven," (Matthew 5:3) sound not idealistic, but revolutionary.

Even coins bore Caesar's image, sparking debates on idolatry. When asked about tribute, *Yeshua* replied, "Give to Caesar what is Caesar's and to God what is God's." (Mark 12:17) A perfect summary of Second Temple tension of navigating public life while guarding divine allegiance. Certain phrases united this era's literature:

- "Light versus Darkness." Derived from Essene hymns, this contrast expressed moral clarity. John's Gospel would later open with identical imagery, "The light shines in the darkness." (John 1:5)

- "Son of Man." From Daniel 7:13: "One like a son of man was coming with the clouds of heaven." To first-century ears, this symbolized heaven-sent authority opposed to earthly beasts (empires). *Yeshua*'s self-identification with this title electrified audiences.

- "Day of *Adonai*" Once a metaphor for judgment upon nations, it became personal and forced the question, when would God vindicate us?

These images gave language for the gospels' proclamation that the time had come, and the kingdom of heaven had drawn near.

Generations under domination cultivated resilience through ritual. *Shabbat* insisted that rest belonged to God, not Rome. Festivals rehearsed rescue annually. Every circumcision reaffirmed covenant continuity. Faith became resistance in rhythm.

This posture of waiting made the appearance of any prophetic voice incredibly magnetic. When shepherds heard angels or fishermen met a wonder-worker who healed lepers, their hearts recognized fulfillment without needing scholarly proof. Expectancy had prepared discernment.

Though sects differed, they converged in yearning for a singular promise of the established Kingdom of God. Not merely territory or politics, this meant a world aligned with divine justice and peace where *shalom* embraced creation. Isaiah 11 painted the vision, "A shoot will come out from the stump of Jesse . . . The Spirit of *Adonai* will rest on Him—the Spirit of wisdom and understanding . . . The wolf will dwell with the lamb." (Isaiah 11:1-6) Every faction saw itself as preparing for that reign. Even their arguments proclaimed belief that God still cared enough to reveal His will. From this era, there are a few lessons for our generation:

1. Diversity can serve destiny. The late Second Temple spectrum illustrates that disagreement, when anchored in reverence, enriches faith. We too can differ without dividing the covenant community.

2. Holiness transcends buildings. *Torah.* True worship persists in the ordinary.

3. Hope must be active. Every group channeled expectation into practice. Study, purity, resistance, and withdrawal were means of covenant fidelity. Faith that waits idly ceases to be faith.

4. The Kingdom belongs to the humble. Movements rose and fell, but the final revelation came through poverty and service. God's reign surprises pride.

Culmination – The Voice in the Wilderness

Among all these voices, one finally captured the nation's heart. "Repent, for the kingdom of heaven is at hand!" (Matthew 3:2) John the Immerser stood at the Jordan River, a location heavy with memory of entry into Promised Land. He immersed multitudes while declaring that ceremonial washings must manifest into inner transformation. He was neither priest nor scholar, Pharisee nor Zealot. Yet all flocked to him. His appearance marked the turning point between expectation and realization.

The Essenes' purity, the Pharisees' teaching, and the Zealots' zeal all met in that flowing river as John proclaimed preparation for One greater than himself. The centuries of Second Temple longing were converging into a single message that proclaimed, "the King is coming."

Looking back, the kaleidoscope of the period forms a divine symphony rather than cacophony. Every movement contributed to a melody. The Pharisees taught the people to love *Torah*. The Sadducees maintained ritual continuity. The Essenes preserved Scripture and purity. The Zealots kept passion for freedom alive. And through the faith of common people, hope never ceased.

Out of their harmonies and dissonances, the ultimate symphony would emerge, the Word made flesh. "The people walking in darkness have seen a great light; those dwelling in the land of the shadow of death, on them light has shined." (Isaiah 9:6) Their hopes, prayers, and arguments prepared that sunrise. Every voice, whether reasoning in synagogue, chanting in cave, or shouting on battlefield, cried for the same dawn. In *Yeshua* the Messiah, that dawn broke.

9

Scrolls by the Dead Sea
Waiting for the End of Days

In 1947 a Bedouin shepherd threw a stone into a cave near the north-western shore of the Dead Sea and heard the shattering of pottery, not empty echo. When he entered, he found jars containing scrolls wrapped in linen. These scrolls contained texts untouched for almost two millennia.

Scholars would soon identify them as the oldest biblical manuscripts ever discovered. These were the Dead Sea Scrolls, and their hiding place was in Qumran. The story of their concealment originated in the final generation before the Roman destruction of 70 CE, but their composition stretched to a time when groups within Israel withdrew from public life, choosing wilderness over compromise. The scrolls they copied preserved not only Scripture but their interpretation of it, their prayers, rules, hymns, and expectations for the End of Days.

Discovery of Qumran did not merely add archaeology to history. It provided us with a time capsule of Second Temple spirituality in its most authentic form, revealing the thoughts of the prophets' descendants as they awaited God's deliverance.

The Desert as Refuge and Revelation

The Dead Sea valley is one of the harshest regions on earth. The valley is below sea-level, ringed by barren cliffs, and its air thick with salt. Yet to ancient Israelites, the wilderness always signified purification and renewal. It was there that Israel first received *Torah*, there Elijah heard God's still small voice, and there Isaiah foresaw a highway for the coming glory. "A voice cries out, 'In the wilderness prepare the way of *Adonai*, make straight in the desert a highway for our God." (Isaiah 40:3)

For Qumran's inhabitants, called by modern scholars the *Yahad*, or "the Community," the desert symbolized separation from impurity and preparation for revelation. They believed that if the world was corrupt, faithfulness required flight, not compromise. So, they built a monastery of stone halls, ritual baths (*mikva'ot*), dining rooms, and scriptorium tables where parchment was cut and copied with reverence.

Most historians trace the group's beginnings to the mid-second century BCE during the Hasmonean era. A priestly faction, outraged by the corruption and Hellenization of Jerusalem High Priesthood, withdrew from the Temple, awaiting divine vindication. They viewed their leader, sometimes called the Teacher of Righteousness, as a prophetic figure standing against a "Wicked Priest" in Jerusalem.[77]

The Community Rule (1QS) outlines their structure. Entry followed a two-year probation, property was shared

---

[77] VanderKam, James C. The Dead Sea Scrolls Today. 2nd ed. Grand Rapids: Eerdmans, 2010, 83–102.

communally, meals were eaten in silence after priestly blessing, and transgressions, even minor ones, resulted in suspension from the communal table. They lived with the rigor of Levites and the anticipation of prophets.

For them, history was sacred drama. Israel at war with spiritual darkness, priesthood corrupted, Gentile rule oppressive, but heaven preparing to intervene. They called this imminent epoch "the Visitation," a divine inspection of humanity and establishment of eternal righteousness.[78]

Excavations at Qumran have uncovered not grandeur but discipline. These excavations reveal rows of small dwellings, large cisterns for ritual washing, communal kitchens, with evidence of writing like inkwells, benches, and scribing tables. Hundreds of clay jars similar to those found filled with scrolls indicate mass textual production.

Nearby cemetery rows contain over 1,000 graves, oriented north–south, reflecting ordered egalitarian burial. Pottery fragments dated around the turn of the era confirm continuous occupation for nearly two centuries until 66 CE. Coin hoards suggest trade with surrounding towns despite ideological isolation. The combination of purity pools and literary output reveals their character as students of Scripture who pursued sanctity through scholarship and self-discipline. Their "monasticism" prefigured later Christian orders, though rooted purely in *Torah* devotion.[79]

Roughly 900 manuscripts were eventually found across eleven caves. These consisted of about two-thirds of the

---

[78] Vermes, Geza, 97–117 (Community Rule 1QS).
[79] Magness, Jodi,

Hebrew Scripture, and the rest were sectarian or apocryphal writings. Among them:

- Biblical Scrolls. Fragments from every book except Esther, often 1,000 years older than the Masoretic text. These confirm the remarkable preservation of Scripture through centuries.
- Apocrypha and Pseudepigrapha. Books like Jubilees, 1 Enoch, Tobit, and Sirach. These works reflecting themes common in Judaism of the era.
- Sectarian Texts. Community Rule, Damascus Document, War Scroll, Thanksgiving Hymns, and *Pesher* (commentary) on Habakkuk, Psalms and others.

Together they form a library of devotion, law, mysticism, and expectation. These were the heartbeat of a people who saw themselves living on the cusp of prophecy's fulfillment.[80]

At the community's theological core was a worldview of stark dualism, light versus darkness and truth versus deceit. They interpreted Deuteronomy 30:15 literally, "See, I have set before you today life and good, and death and evil." Humanity stood divided between "the Prince of Light" and the "Angel of Darkness."

This battle was not mythic fantasy. Instead, it was personal ethics. Every thought and deed indicated allegiance to one dominion or the other. The Community Rule proclaims, "To each man *Adonai* has allotted two spirits . . . the Spirit of Truth and the Spirit of Deceit." They understood history as a countdown toward decisive

---

[80] VanderKam, James C., 43–64.

judgment when the sons of light would triumph. Hence their obsession with purity. Without personal holiness, one might inadvertently strengthen darkness.[81]

Daily immersions in *mikva'ot* symbolized internal cleansing.[82] Meals mirrored Temple offerings while their bread and wine were blessed like sacrifices. Because they considered the Jerusalem priests defiled, every act replicated Temple worship in miniature. Qumran itself became a portable Sanctuary that awaited the arrival of the heavenly one.

Within the scrolls, the mysterious Teacher of Righteousness looms large. He was described as one whom "God made known all the mysteries of His servants, the prophets." Apparently, he suffered persecution and perhaps martyrdom at the hands of the wicked priestly establishment.

---

[81] Martínez, Florentino García, and Eibert J. C. Tigchelaar, eds. *The Dead Sea Scrolls Study Edition*. 2 vols. Leiden: Brill, 1997–1998, 88-89.
[82] In the Second Temple period, immersion in a mikveh was a common and meaningful act of purification practiced throughout the land, especially in and around Jerusalem and communities like Qumran. These stepped pools, filled with "living water" (*mayim chayim*), invited the worshiper to descend physically and spiritually from a state of impurity toward renewal. Before entering, a person carefully removed anything that might block contact with the water, ensuring complete immersion. With deliberate steps, the individual descended into the mikveh until fully submerged, allowing the water to envelop the entire body. For a moment beneath the surface, one symbolically passed from impurity to purity. This act was never merely external. Texts like the Community Rule emphasize that immersion without repentance was insufficient. True cleansing required a turning of the heart. As such, the mikveh embodied teshuvah—a return to God—and a renewal of covenant faithfulness. Emerging from the water, the individual was considered restored and prepared to reenter sacred life. Each immersion pointed beyond itself, anticipating the promised day when God would fully cleanse His people and dwell among them.

For the community, his suffering modeled fidelity amid corruption. This was a prototype of the righteous sufferer from Isaiah 53, "He was despised and rejected by men, a man of sorrows and acquainted with grief." [83] Many scholars see this as early development of the concept later fulfilled perfectly in *Yeshua*. The Teacher was not divine but exemplary. His role was to prepare hearts for the final revelation. His memory changed despair into perseverance that illustrated how God always raises teachers to interpret His silence.

Among the most dramatic of their writings is the War Scroll (1QM), outlining a seven-stage cosmic conflict between "the Sons of Light" and "the Sons of Darkness." It details trumpets of assembly, battle formations, priestly blessings before combat, and angelic partnership. The victory ends with universal peace under God's reign. This militarized spirituality shows the apocalyptic imagination of the time where even peace required purgation. They envisioned themselves as the faithful remnant destined to participate in God's ultimate triumph, wielding holiness instead of politics to conquer evil.[84]

Counterbalancing militant imagery is profound humility. The Thanksgiving Hymns reveal individual prayer like expanded Psalms, brimming with contrition and awe, "I thank You, O Lord, for You have redeemed my soul from the pit, and from *Sheol Abaddon* You have raised me to everlasting height." (1QHa) These hymns echo

---

[83] Martínez, Florentino García, 75-83

[84] Collins, John J. *The Apocalyptic Imagination: An Introduction to Jewish Apocalyptic Literature*, 3rd ed. (Grand Rapids: Eerdmans, 2016), 147–150.

Psalm 40 and Psalm 103, yet with heightened introspection. They present humanity as dust enlightened only by grace. These are remarkably close to New Covenant language decades later.[85]

Covenant Renewal – A Community of the Last Days

Membership in the sect required oath binding every aspect of life to the covenant. Participants swore "to seek God with whole heart and soul, to do what is good and right before Him." Their annual ceremony of re-enlistment included reading blessings for obedience and curses for transgression which mirrored Deuteronomy 27-28. They called themselves "the New Covenant of the Land of Damascus. "This moniker was based on Jeremiah 31:31, "Behold, days are coming . . . when I will make a new covenant with the house of Israel." While not the same covenant later inaugurated by Messiah, their appropriation shows intense desire for renewed relationship. Covenant theology was no abstraction. But instead, it was their daily identity.[86]

Unique to Qumran are the *pesher* commentaries. These commentaries provided verse-by-verse explanations of Hebrew scriptures applying prophetic texts directly to their times. They interpreted Habakkuk, Isaiah, and Psalms as coded messages about current rulers and events. The word *pesher* (interpretation) appears repeatedly, "This is the *pesher* of the word . . ." For example, Habakkuk's rebuke of proud oppressors was read as

---

85 VanderKam, James C. 104–108.
86 Ibid., 97–104.

prophecy of their own generation's priests and foreign overlords. They believed revelation was ongoing while prophecy spoke "again" whenever the community read it. This concept of Scripture as living word reshaped Jewish and later Christian hermeneutics. When apostles reinterpreted Psalms or Isaiah to describe Messiah, they followed this same *midrashic* instinct.[87]

The Community lived by a strict timetable. Each day included sunrise prayers, ritual baths, work (copying, farming, pottery), sunset assembly, and shared meal. Every act acknowledged divine sovereignty. Before eating bread, the priest blessed God for "fruits of the earth." After the meal, they recited thanksgiving psalms and prayers. This rhythm infused holiness into survival chores. Thus, echoing the creation pattern that order was formed from chaos.

Infractions such as anger, gossip, and tardiness to prayer were penalized. Yet forgiveness was possible through repentance and extra purification. Their manual insists, "When these things happen in Israel, reconciling in love . . . then the congregation shall be established forever." Spiritually, Qumran was both a strict school and family.[88]

Evidence suggests that some Essene groups were celibate, but others, like those described by Josephus north of Ein Gedi, allowed families. At Qumran proper, most graves are male, hinting that its specific branch emphasized celibacy as purity which later anticipated monastic traditions. Women elsewhere nonetheless played

---

[87] Ibid., 111–115.
[88] Ibid., 96–104.

key roles in sustaining Essene settlements through agricultural and trade networks.

Their renunciation of marriage was not contempt for creation but protest against priestly corruption tied to inheritance and property. By cutting lineage ties, they freed devotion from politics. Their goal was spiritual rebirth as "Children of Light," transcending social hierarchies.[89]

How They Read the Prophets

The scrolls show unprecedented reverence for Isaiah, Deuteronomy, and Psalms. These are the texts that define covenant, purity, and Messianic promise. One Isaiah manuscript (1QIsaʿa) preserves the entire book almost intact, confirming prophetic centrality. Messianic references appear everywhere as a branch from David, an anointed priest, and a coming prophet. One fragment (4Q521) proclaims, "The heavens and earth will listen to His Messiah . . . The poor will be satisfied with good things, He will heal the wounded, give life to the dead, proclaim good news to the poor."

These lines, older than the Gospels, ring astonishingly familiar to Luke 7:22, where *Yeshua* answers John's question using identical phrases. Thus, the Qumran texts reveal the theological atmosphere of a world already yearning for such signs.[90]

---

[89] Ibid., 94–96, 110–112.
[90] Collins, John J. *The Scepter and the Star: Messianism in Light of the Dead Sea Scrolls*, 131–135.

Qumran and the New Testament World

Though the sect withdrew from society, its influence quietly permeated. John the Immerser's desert asceticism parallels their ethos of an immersion for repentance, a voice in the wilderness, and an expectation of imminent judgment. Scholars debate whether John had contact with them. If not, their proximity demonstrates shared scriptural interpretation.

Yeshua's message, however, redirected their rigidity toward compassion. Where they built walls, He built bridges. Their prayers begged deliverance for "Children of Light." He extended the title to all who believe. Their exclusivity became His inclusivity, fulfilling Isaiah 49:6, "I will also give You as a light to the nations." In essence, *Yeshua* stepped into the same apocalyptic horizon but revealed that the long-expected Kingdom arrived not through holy war but through holy love.

Before Qumran, the oldest Hebrew manuscripts dated over a millennium later. The scrolls' discovery validated the integrity of the biblical text preserved by scribes. For example, Isaiah 53 appears word-for-word consistent with later manuscripts except for minor spelling differences. This consistency attested to God's preservation of Scripture. The psalms collection mirrors the canonical order, confirming ancient liturgical use. Variants illuminate interpretive nuance without altering theology. These findings strengthened confidence that when *Yeshua* and His disciples quoted Scripture, they drew from essentially the same text we read today.[91]

The Timeless Human Questions at Qumran

Why does evil persist? How can the righteous endure corruption around them? When will God act? In Qumran's caves we hear those questions carved into scrolls. And though their timeline proved mistaken, the world did not end in their lifetime, their yearning was faithful. They teach that waiting for redemption is itself an act of worship.

Their dualistic worldview may appear rigid, yet morally it confronts our comfortable relativism. For them there were no neutral deeds. Every choice pushed creation either toward light or darkness. That conviction, filtered through *Yeshua*'s ethic of love, becomes enduring truth: every act participates in kingdom or chaos.

When Roman troops advanced in 68 CE, Qumranites hid their library in caves expecting to retrieve it after victory. They never returned. Yet their failure became our fortune, and their clay jars preserved voices that would have been lost. Those parchments, carried by desert wind and time, now rest in climate-controlled cases in Jerusalem, still declaring holiness.

Their faithfulness outlived their predictions. They believed the world would end, but instead, their words endured 2,000 years to remind believers that Scripture

---

[91] Abegg, Martin. Peter Flint, and Eugene Ulrich, *The Dead Sea Scrolls Bible* (New York: HarperOne, 1999), 8–15.

never ends. "The grass withers, the flower fades, but the word of our God stands forever." (Isaiah 40:8)

Modern Echoes: Living as Sons of Light

Reading Qumran today challenges spiritual complacency. Their radical separation asks us, "What does it mean to live distinct from corruption while remaining engaged with mercy?" *Yeshua* prayed, "They are not of the world, just as I am not of the world. Sanctify them in the truth—Your word is truth." (John 17.16-17)

That tension, being in yet not of the world, defines faithful discipleship still. We need not imitate their isolation, but we should emulate their intensity to memorize Scripture, to be a disciplined community, and to maintain hope fiercely. To be a "Son of Light" today is to shine ethical clarity into confusion, to resist moral compromise with acts of compassion, and to keep lamps burning amid cultural night. Those in Qumran extend lessons for every generation:

1. Holiness Without Hate. Separation must protect purity without breeding contempt. Qumran's fall warns that withdrawal can freeze compassion. Holiness is relational, not solitary.
2. Study as Worship. Their scribal labor was liturgy. So too, every believer's engagement with Scripture can become prayer. To write, read, or teach the Word is to extend their legacy of devotion.
3. Hope Beyond Headlines. Apocalyptic fears resurface in every era. Qumran reminds us that

God's timeline is purposeful, not predictable. Faith watches and works, not speculates.

4. The Faithful Remnant. *Adonai* always preserves a community that clings to His covenant. Their cave hymns echo Elijah's discovery, "I have kept for Myself 7,000 in Israel, all whose knees have not bowed to Baal." (1 Kings 19:18)

5. Scripture's Preservation of Promise. The survival of their scrolls is itself a miracle testifying that divine revelation cannot be silenced by history.

The men of Qumran rose each dawn believing they lived in the final generation. Perhaps every faithful generation should believe the same, not to calculate dates but to cultivate readiness. They wrote, "When these things begin to happen, the eternal light shall shine to the limits of the world."[92] Their hope was not naïve. Instead, it was a vow that God's justice will indeed illuminate creation. For believers in Messiah, that light has already dawned.

Paul would later echo their vocabulary, "For you are all sons of light and sons of day—we are not of night nor of darkness." (1Thessalonians 5:5) He transformed their sectarian slogan into universal calling. Through Messiah, every nation may join the company of light.

Epilogue – The Scrolls Still Speak

From their silent caves the Dead Sea Scrolls now whisper across millennia. Be pure when the world is

---

[92] Collins, John J. *The Apocalyptic Imagination: An Introduction to Jewish Apocalyptic Literature*, 141–145.

polluted. Be faithful when the Temple crumbles. Be studious when prophets seem scarce. Be hopeful when heaven appears delayed. Their ink has faded, but their witness endures as a chorus reminding us that revelation is not a relic but a living covenant.

In their longing for the End of Days, the Qumran community unknowingly prepared the world for the advent of *Yeshua HaMachiach*, the Light who entered their darkness and ours. "The people walking in darkness have seen a great light. Those dwelling in the shadow of death— light has dawned." (Isaiah 9:1)

10

Messiah and the Temple
Expectation Fulfilled

All through Israel's history one yearning that God would dwell among His people again in visible power defined their faith. From Moses' Tent of Meeting to Solomon's Temple, from exile to rebuilding, the refrain persisted. "Return, *Adonai*, to Your resting place." (Psalm 132:8) But the prophetic writers promised more than a building. They foresaw a day when heaven and earth would meet within a single Anointed One, a living sanctuary. Isaiah spoke of Immanuel, Micah prophesied of a ruler from Bethlehem, and Malachi predicted a messenger who would visit the Temple suddenly. Generations waited expectantly.

Now, as Herod's massive marble Temple glimmered across the Mount of Olives, ordinary men and women prayed in its courtyards unaware that the very Presence they sought had been born among them.

The Temple of Herod as Stage for Revelation

By the first decades of the first century CE, Herod's reconstruction project had turned Jerusalem into one of the architectural marvels of the Roman world. White limestone terraces rose above the city, visible for miles. But its apparent permanence masked deep unrest with the presence of Roman occupation, priestly corruption, social inequality, and apocalyptic expectation.

Into this atmosphere came *Yeshua* of Nazareth, a Galilean craftsman steeped in Scripture. His life unfolded as a quiet commentary on the Temple's rituals, symbols, and purposes, finding new significance in Him.

Luke records His family's early pilgrimage, "When eight days had passed . . . they brought Him up to Jerusalem to present Him to *Adonai*." (Luke 2:21-22) Within those same courts, aged Simeon, moved by the *Ruach HaKodesh*, took the infant in his arms and declared, "My eyes have seen Your salvation." (Luke 2:30) The Temple that longed for Messiah was literally holding Him.

At twelve, *Yeshua* returned for Passover, separated from His parents, and was found debating teachers, "Did you not know that I must be in My Father's House?" (Luke 2:49) Already He defined the Temple not as human stronghold but relational meeting point. It was the Father's dwelling even if priests barely perceived it.

Nearly thirty years later, John the Immerser's ministry at the Jordan stirred thousands. When *Yeshua* entered those waters, heaven opened, the *Ruach* descended like a dove, and a voice proclaimed, "This is My Son, whom I love; with Him I am well pleased." (Matthew 3:17)

The presence that had once filled Solomon's Temple now rested upon *Yeshua* Himself. He was the new dwelling place of divine glory. A living Temple among His people. Every miracle and parable from that point forward streamed from the conviction that what the Temple symbolized, He embodied.

Not long after beginning His public ministry, He ascended to Jerusalem for Passover. There He saw merchants and money changers exploiting worshipers within the outer courts reserved for the nations. He overturned their tables, saying, "My House shall be called a House of Prayer, but you have made it a den of robbers!" (Mark 11:17, quoting Isaiah 56:7 and Jeremiah 7:11)

This was no random act of anger. It was prophetic theater. Jeremiah had once uttered the same words before Babylon's invasion. *Yeshua* signaled that Jerusalem's leadership was repeating history. The cleansing bore both mercy and warning. God desired repentance before judgment. The Sadducean elite viewed blasphemy as a grave offense. They believed that the Temple's economy was essential for their survival, but to God, it represented a betrayal of the covenant. Thus began the deadly conflict between institutional religion and living revelation.

Gospels portray *Yeshua* repeatedly in the Temple teaching parables, healing the blind and lame, and receiving children's praise fulfilling Isaiah 35:5-6, "Then the eyes of the blind will be opened, the lame will leap like a dear." Every healing enacted prophecy. Crowds marveled while the priests plotted. Even as opposition mounted, He kept calling the building "My Father's house." His words reframed access to God away from ritual and toward relationship, "The Son does nothing by Himself, but only what He sees the Father doing." (John 5:19) In effect, He carried Temple holiness wherever He went and where He stood, heaven touched earth. Throughout His ministry, *Yeshua* included imagery of the Temple in His teachings:

1. Prayer and Presence. He taught disciples to pray facing heaven rather than architecture: "Our Father in heaven, sanctified be Your name." (Matthew 6:9) Sanctity shifted from place to relationship.

2. Forgiveness and Sacrifice. Sermon on the Mount recalled altar practice, "If you are bringing your gift to the altar and remember your brother has something against you, leave your gift there . . . first be reconciled with your brother." (Matthew 5:23-24) He transposed ritual into ethics and promoted reconciliation as the higher offering.

3. Light of the World. During the Feast of Tabernacles, enormous lamps illuminated Temple courts. Standing there *Yeshua* declared, "I am the light of the world." (John 8:12) The people who once watched flames recalling wilderness fire now saw its fulfillment in His eyes.

4. Living Water. At the same feast priests poured water at the altar praying for rain. He cried, "If anyone is thirsty, let him come to Me and drink! Whoever believes in Me, as the Scripture say, out of his innermost being will flow rivers of living water." (John 7:37-38) He transformed liturgical act into the spiritual reality of the Spirit as an eternal fountain. Through such sayings, *Yeshua* became a

living Temple, and each ritual was performed by a person instead of a place.

At another Passover, watching His zeal, some demanded a sign of authority. He answered enigmatically, "Destroy this temple, and in three days I will raise it up." (John 2:19) They mocked saying, "Forty-six years has this temple been built, and will You raise it in three days?" John clarifies, "He was speaking about the temple of His body." (John 2:21). The mortal body as the divine dwelling is presented as the axis of the new covenant. When the veil of His flesh was torn on the cross, the Temple veil itself ripped from top to bottom (Matthew 27:51). Presence burst from confinement into every heart.

On His final approach to Jerusalem, descending the Mount of Olives, He wept over the city, "If only you had recognized this day the things that lead to *shalom*! But now they are hidden from your eyes. For days will come upon you when your enemies . . . will not leave one stone upon another, because you did not recognize the time of your visitation." (Luke 19:42-44) The phrase "time of your visitation" echoed Qumran's expectation of divine inspection. [93] *Yeshua* declared it fulfilled, but He was rejected. His lament fused priestly compassion with prophetic sorrow. In Matthew 24 He predicted explicitly, "Do you see all these things? Amen, I tell you, not one stone will be left upon another." The building project meant to immortalize faith would fall within a generation.

[93] Schiffman, Lawrence H. *Reclaiming the Dead Sea Scrolls* (Philadelphia: Jewish Publication Society, 1994), 214–218.

During His last week, *Yeshua* shared Passover with His disciples in a Jerusalem upper room where He transformed the liturgy into covenant renewal. "After taking *matzah* and giving thanks, He broke it and gave to them, saying, 'This is My body, given for you. Do this in memory of Me.' He took the cup . . . saying, 'This cup is the new covenant in My blood." (Luke 22:19-20)

The new altar became the table and the new sacrifice, Himself. As a priest once sprinkled blood on mercy seat, so His own blood would open mercy for the world. That night, arrested and abused, He stood before the high priest who demanded, "Are You the Messiah, the Son of the Blessed One?" *Yeshua* replied, "I am, and you will see the Son of Man sitting at the right hand of Power and coming with the clouds of heaven." (Mark 14:61-62) He quoted Daniel 7, the very apocalyptic text loved by Qumran's watchers. The claim placed Him as both King and Priest in a single person. The role no Hasmonean could righteously hold.

The Crucifixion – The Veil Torn

As he hung on the cross outside the city walls, priests were slaughtering Passover lambs inside the temple. At the same hour, he uttered, "It is finished." (John 19:30) the Greek term *teleōo* implies completion of purpose a perfect offering. Immediately, "and behold, the veil of the temple was split into from top to bottom." (Matthew 27:51)

The barrier between God and all humanity collapsed. Herod's architectural glory had been irrelevant while heaven's glory entered hearts. *Yeshua*, rejected by the priesthood, became the heavenly High Priest for all "after the order of Melchizedek." (Psalm 110:4; Hebrew 7:17)

On the third day, the prophecy bound to His identity came true. The Temple of his body was raised. The angels announced, "He is not here, for he has been raised just as He said." (Matthew 28:6)

When the disciples encountered Him, they stood upon the very truth that God is dwelling with us! The *Shekhinah* that once filled the Holy of Holies now filled flesh. From that resurrection flowed a new axis of worship that was no longer limited by country or geography. The risen Temple would soon ascend and pour out *Ruach HaKodesh* upon believers.

Fifty days later, on *Shavuot* (Pentecost), tongues of fire descended upon gathered disciples in Jerusalem. God's own architecture shifted once for all. Living souls became living stones for a new Temple. Peter proclaimed Joel's prophecy, "I will pour out my *Ruach* on all flesh." (Joel 3:1) A kingdom never to be destroyed began quietly among 120 souls. Paul later crystallized revelation, "Do you not know that you are God's temple and that the *Ruach Elohim* dwells in you?" (1 Corinthians 3:16) "For we are all the temple of the living God." (2 Corinthians 6:16) What Ezekiel envisioned and Qumran sought, the spirit accomplished. Humanity became the dwelling place of God.

The apostles continued to pray in Herod's courts (Acts 2:46; 3:1). They healed a lame man at its gate beautiful, echoing Isaiah 35 again. But opposition soon arose. Stephen's bold speech declared, "The Most High does not dwell in houses made by hands. (Acts 7:48) His martyrdom signified the coming break between stone and Spirit.

As decades passed, Rome tightened its grip. Rebellions flared and false messiahs multiplied. In 66 CE the Great Revolt erupted, culminating in 70 CE with Titus's legions surrounding Jerusalem. The Temple burned again as *Yeshua* foretold. Josephus records that priests clinging to the altar were consumed in flames. As the flames grew gold melted between stones, displaying a grim mirror of Herod's earlier splendor. But the faith of Messiah's followers endured. They had learned that the true Temple Had already risen.[94]

The Fulfillment of Every Symbol

Every golden vessel found its living counterpart. Thus, the Temple's destruction did not end worship. Instead, its worship was transferred it into eternity. Heaven no longer waits behind a veil but walks within believers. Through the ministry of *Yeshua*, the Temple was symbolically replaced from place to person to people:

1. From Place to Person. God's dwelling moved from mountain to tent to temple to Messiah Himself.

2. From Person to People. Through Spirit, His indwelling spreads to all who believe. The body of Messiah is now "a holy priesthood offering spiritual sacrifices acceptable to God." (1 Peter 2:5)

---

[94] Mason, Steve trans., *The Jewish War* by Josephus (Peabody, MA: Hendrickson, 2016), 391–395.

3. From People to Cosmos. Revelation 21 completes the journey, "I saw no temple in the city, for the Lord God Almighty and the Lamb are its Temple."

History is moving toward universal indwelling. The creation as a sanctuary. Thus, giving profound implications for faith and life:

1. Worship Without Walls. Every place, classroom, home, market, synagogue, and church, becomes holy when saturated with His Presence.

2. Holiness of the Heart. External rituals find meaning only as internal truth. Morality is our incense while compassion is our offering.

3. Continuous Dedication. Just as priests daily trimmed lamps, believers daily tend the Spirit's flame through prayer and obedience.

4. Hope of restoration. Jewish and Christian faith alike cling to a prophetic vision of a Temple restored and the Messianic age. Yet they realize its essence already exists within.

After Pentecost, Jerusalem's believers still honored temple rhythms. *Shabbat*, festivals, and prayer hours were covenant markers that sanctified them. However, they interpreted them through *Yeshua*. Breaking bread in homes reenacted his sacrifice, and sacrificial terminology permeated praise. They did not see themselves as abandoning Judaism but fulfilling it. Their hearts became a living sanctuary where the *Shekinah* dwelt once more. This fusion of temple symbolism and spiritual experience set the foundation for centuries of Messianic and Christian worship. The continuation of Isaiah's dream, "A House of prayer for all nations."

Prophets foresee a future restoration, not of a stone political building alone but of divine presence filling earth. Ezekiel 47 describes living waters flowing from a future Temple to heal the Dead Sea. The symbol of life overflowing desolation. Revelation 22 fulfills it, "The river of the water of life, clear as crystal flowing from the throne of God and of the Lamb."

The end of Scripture returns to its beginning. Eden reopened, and God tabernacling with humanity. "Behold the dwelling of God is with men." (Revelation 21:3) The cosmos itself becomes the Temple. *Yeshua* is the corner stone of this eternal structure. Its blueprint is founded on love where no fire can destroy it, and no empire can occupy it.

Reflection – The Temple and Your Heart

The ancients built altars of stone. Today, we build altars of time and attention. Every prayer, every act of mercy, and every moment of repentance lays another brick within the living temple. If Qumran's priests awaited the day of visitation, we await the day of completion when the lamb returns in glory. Until then, *Yeshua*'s words guide our watchfulness, "Be ready, for the son of man is coming at an hour you do not expect."

To live in readiness is to keep the lamp of faith trimmed and burning, to speak truth in love, and to forgive as we are forgiven. We are to stand as priests of mercy in a world in need of holiness. Then the prophecy becomes real in each soul, "For the glory of *Adonai* has risen upon you." (Isaiah 60:1)

Epilogue – Expectation Fulfilled, Expectation Continues

The Temple stood for centuries as a promise of God with us. In *Yeshua*, that promise was fulfilled. His promise has not ended but deepened. His Spirit still streams through deserts of unbelief, while building altars in ordinary hearts. The final fire tore Jerusalem's veil, but a greater light rose in its place.

To study the Second Temple is to trace the long path of God's patience. To meet Messiah in its history is to see that patience reaches its goal. The House of *Adonai* has indeed been rebuilt one soul at a time. "And the city has no need of the sun or the moon to shine on it, for the glory of God lights it up, and its lamp is the Lamb. (Revelation 21:23) The Temple is fulfilled and the Lamb is its light. History still echoes with the invitation to come and be the dwelling of God.

Part IV: Destruction and New Life

11

The Last Stand

The Fall of Jerusalem

By the middle of the first century CE, Judea simmered. The marble courtyards that Herod built glittered outwardly, but corruption and anxiety festered underneath. The earlier Hasmoneans had blended priesthood and monarchy. Now Rome had achieved domination, and appointed client kings and governors who taxed mercilessly.

Economically, Rome demanded tribute on land and produce. Politically, it placed pagan symbols on military standards even near the Temple precincts. For a nation whose worship centered on separation from idolatry, this was salt in deep wounds.

The "Pax Romana," peace of Rome, meant silence through fear. Small uprisings had flared like the Galilean revolt under Judas the Zealot (6 CE) but were crushed with brutality. Resentment among the Jews only deepened. Pilgrims poured into Jerusalem during the festival seasons. Every spring, during Passover, the festival of liberation from Egypt, rekindled longing for liberation from Rome. Each year the empire tightened its watch, and each year Jewish hope pressed harder against the cage.

Sparks before the Storm (44–66 CE)

Roman procurators rarely understood Jewish custom. The governor Cumanus allowed Greek soldiers to mock pilgrims during Passover, triggering riot and massacre. His successor, Felix, turned suppression into opportunity, hiring assassins to eliminate rivals. Another governor, Florus (64–66 CE), plundered the Temple treasury under pretense of collecting imperial tax.[95]

Josephus records, "The whole nation was inflamed, and madness seized the people."[96] Citizens gathered in protests. Florus responded by crucifying Jews within sight of the city walls. The horror burst the dam. Even as outrage spread, factions within Israel divided responses.

- The Zealots, descendants of, Judas the Galilean, argued that continued payment of tribute violated God's kingship.
- The Sadducees and priestly elite depended on Rome and preached patience.
- The Pharisees promoted spiritual reform rather than violent rebellion.
- The majority merely wanted peace and harvest without interference.

But collective humiliation over the Temple's desecration united extremes. Rumor spread that angels had appeared above the altar promising divine help. National pride ignited into holy war.

The Outbreak of Revolt (66 CE)

In August 66 CE, rebellion began in Caesarea Maritima, the Roman provincial capital, when Greeks sacrificed birds in front of a synagogue that served as a deliberate

---

[95] Ibid., 259–262, 284–289.
[96] Flavius Josephus, *The Jewish War*, trans. G. A. Williamson, rev. E. Mary Smallwood, 134–136.

provocation. The local protest spiraled into street battle, and Roman authorities ignored pleas for justice.

Soon after, Jerusalem radicals seized power. The priest *Eleazar ben Ananis*, effectively declaring independence, stopped sacrifices offered for Caesar in the Temple. It was an unprecedented, open rejection of Rome's authority.

Zealot factions raided the Antonia Fortress, slaughtered soldiers, and captured immense stores of weaponry. The Roman garrison capitulated under promise of safety but was massacred as it left the city. A definite atrocity that ensured Rome's fury. The revolt spread across Galilee under the leadership of *Yosef ben Matityahu*, governor of the region on behalf of the provisional government. He will be later known, ironically, as Josephus, historian for Rome. Rome's response was swift and merciless. Emperor Nero sent seasoned general Vespasian and his son Titus with three legions, over 60,000 troops, plus auxiliary forces and siege engineers. They advanced systematically. First the Romans subdued Galilee. Then they pressed south toward Jerusalem.[97]

In 67 CE, Roman forces besieged towns fortified by zealots. At Jotapata, after 47 days of siege, resistance collapsed. Joesphus, trapped inside a cave with surviving soldiers, persuaded them to cast lots for suicide so only one might remain alive. He survived, surrendered, and foretold to Vespasian that he would become emperor. This prophecy proved true two years later.

The capture of Galilee left Judea isolated. Refugees fled to Jerusalem, carrying tales of massacre and vengeance.

---

[97] Ibid., 136–140, 156–159, 189–192.

Famine began even before the siege. Inside the city, chaos reigned. Several militant groups fought each other:

- The Zealots, led by John of Giscala and Eleazar ben Simon.
- Idumean auxiliaries who invaded under the pretext of protecting the Temple.
- Priests and moderates seeking peace.

Between them, anarchy prevailed. Stores of grain were burned in internal sabotage, anticipating Rome's siege. Josephus later lamented, "No foreign army so harmed us as those within our own walls."

By 68 CE the revolt had devoured its own heart. Then Rome, momentarily halted by Nero's suicide and civil war, found new momentum when Vespasian indeed became emperor. He entrusted the final campaign to his son, Titus.[98]

The Siege of Jerusalem (70 CE)

In April 70 CE, Titus encircled Jerusalem with the Fifteenth, Twelfth, Fifth, and Tenth legions. It was Passover again and pilgrims swelled the city, doubling the number of mouths to feed. For Roman strategy, this was perfect. He allowed no one to exit, ensuring that starvation would do battles work.

He ordered massive earthen ramparts and siege towers built outside the first and second walls while catapults hurled stones and burning pitch. The zealots fought like cornered lions, believing divine aid was imminent. Messianic prophets declared visions of angels on the walls

---

[98] Ibid., 204–240, 302–306.

as hunger turned those prophecies to delirium. Lamentations 1:12 echoed their anguish, "Is it nothing to you who passed by? Look and see if there is any pain like my pain!"

Josephus writes that families hoarded crumbs, neighbors stole from one another, mothers snatched food from their babies. People gnawed on leather and grass. Prophecies of Deuteronomy 28 regarding siege found terrifying literalness. Moral collapse matched physical desolation.

Outside the walls stood the crosses. Romans crucified all they captured, up to hundreds per day, until no wood remained. From Golgotha to Mount Olive hillsides grew forests of corpses. Amid such horror Titus offered amnesty to those who would surrender, but zealots slaughtered them as traitors. Despair reigned.

June the Romans breached the second wall and pressed toward the Temple Mount. Inside, John of Giscala's forces and Eleazar's priests turned courts into fortresses and slaughterhouses.

Titus reportedly did not initially desire to destroy the Temple. Its beauty impressed even pagans. He proposed submission with guarantees of safety. But fanatics answered by burning Roman battering rams and killing their own countrymen seeking peace.

On the 9th of *Av*, ironically the anniversary of Babylon's destruction of the First Temple, a Roman soldier flung a torch through a golden plated window. The cedar beams ignited. Flames rose higher than Herod's colonnades. Priests screamed, trying to rescue sacred vessels while molten gold flowed between cracks of stone. Titus ordered the flames be extinguished, but madness carried both armies. The sanctuary collapsed in a fire as soldiers removed stones to retrieve the melted gold that lay between them. All fulfilling the words of *Yeshua*, "Not one stone will be left upon another." A population once called a Kingdom of Priests now lay enslaved. Those taken captive, 97,000 says Josephus, were marched to Rome. The Temple treasures entered Caesar's house. Immortalized on Titus's arch was the gold menorah and silver trumpets as they were paraded through Roman streets beneath the shouts of triumph.

Of nearly a million souls Josephus claimed perished, perhaps exaggerated but symbolically true, the nation bled to its foundation. The survivors were sold into slavery or dispersed through the empire. Fortress Masada endured until 73 CE, where its defenders chose death over capture. The Romans renamed the province "Palestina," hoping to erase Judah's memory.[99]

The Pharisaic Legacy and Birth of Rabbinic Judaism

When the smoke lifted, Pharisaic teachers regathered at Yavneh under *Rabban Yochanan ben Zakkai*. His famous petition to Vespasian, "Give me Yavneh and its sages," preserved *Torah* learning. There they re-centered life around Scripture, prayer, and community instead of sacrifice.[100] Judaism's spiritual resilience rose from ashes, "For My people will never be shamed." (Joel 2:26)

Synagogue and home replaced Temple and altar. The *Kaddish* prayer added a line still recited today, "May He

---

[99] Ibid., 311–314, 348–353, 372–377, 391–393.
[100] Shaye J. D. Cohen, 214–219.

establish His kingdom speedily and in our days." Out of devastation grew the long-term hope for rebuilding and the Messiah's return.[101]

Followers of *Yeshua* interpreted the events through His prophecies. Church tradition says they heeded His warnings to flee when Jerusalem was surrounded (Luke 21:20) and escaped to Pella in the Transjordan. Through grieving the Temple's loss, they saw in it validation of a new covenant not dependent on sacrificial system. The Gospel's spread throughout the empire accelerated even as Zion smoldered. Thus, from the same event, two lines emerged, rabbinic Judaism and the Messianic movement. Each movement carried memories of the Temple but interpreting its meaning differently. One view awaited rebuilding while the other proclaimed fulfillment in a living Messiah.[102]

The ashes of 70 CE mark not only political catastrophe but a spiritual turning point. When Solomon dedicated the first Temple he prayed, "If your people sin and you send them into exile, if they pray toward this house, hear from heaven and forgive." (2 Chronicles 6:36-39) That petition resounded again as prayers faced ruin. Rabbi Eliezer later taught, "Since the temple was destroyed the only atonement left is acts of loving-kindness."[103] For Messianic believers the atonement had already been made, and the task was to stand in the mercy born from it.

---

[101] Ibid., 219–223.

[102] Eusebius, *Ecclesiastical History*, trans. G. A. Williamson, 127–129.

[103] *Avot de-Rabbi Natan*, Version A, chap. 4, in Judah Goldin, trans., *The Fathers According to Rabbi Nathan* (New Haven: Yale University Press, 1955), 29–30.

God, once confined to a specific nation and place, was now everywhere his people kneeled. In this sense the destruction did not end God's story with Israel but spread his presence across nations. These historical events have provided valuable reflections:

1. Faith is stronger than stone. Every empire that raised its standard over Jerusalem is gone. Only the people of Israel remain. Rubble proved incapable of silencing holy memory.

2. Prophecy is not revenge. *Yeshua*'s prediction of the Temple's fall was not cursed but mourning. He wept before he warned. True prophets announced judgment with tears, not triumph

3. Exile is a classroom, not a coffin. Like Babylon before, this catastrophe drove faith inward and upward. Prayer became a portable temple and study became sacrifice. Suffering proved seed for survival.

4. Hope never burns out. Each *Tisha b'Av* Jews still fast, chant Lamentations, and end with the words, "Next year in Jerusalem." Every year that sentence defies history's ashes and proclaims faiths flames

Echoes in Stone – Archaeological Testimonies

Modern excavations at the southwestern corner of the temple mount uncovered massive stones hurled by Roman engines still resting where they fell. Their charred edges speak voiceless sermons. The arch of Titus in Rome still depicts soldiers carrying the menorah. Its curved arms serve as a reminder and promise. Jewish pilgrims visiting Rome in later centuries refused to walk beneath that arch, declaring by their detour that Israel's story was not finished. [104] True enough, nineteen centuries later, the *menorah* again stands engraved on the seal of modern Israel. It's a national symbol born from imperial mockery.

History testifies that loss is never final in God's plan. Exile from Zion scattered his word to every continent. Through diaspora communities, the knowledge of *Adonai* entered the nation as scripture and so on. Even now pilgrims press their hands against Herod's remaining retaining stones of the Western Wall while praying for restoration and redemption. Each tear that falls there joins the stream of ancient lament, and heaven still hears. "If I forget you O Jerusalem let my right hand forget its skill." (Psalm 137:5)

The Temple's destruction pushed both Judaism and the Messianic movement to maturity beyond ritual dependency. The revelation that God's house can burn while his promise stands unchanged became permanent theology. For Jews, *Torah* became portable holiness. For believers in *Yeshua* the spirit became indwelling holiness. Both streams affirmed that *Adonai* is faithful even when mountains fall. Their paths diverged but their testimony converged. God's covenant cannot burn.

Prophets and apostles together envision ultimate restoration. Zechariah promised, "Many nations will join themselves to *Adonai* in that day and will become my people." (Zechariah 2:15) Revelation fulfills it with a healed Jerusalem, where no tear remains and no Roman

---

[104] Fine, Steven. *The Arch of Titus: From Jerusalem to Rome—and Back* (Cambridge: Harvard University Press, 2016), 55–62, 132–135.

legion can approach, History's ruin becomes the foundation of eternal peace.

When we walk among the ruins of 70 CE, we stand between judgment and promise. Stone crumbles beneath our hands, but the Spirit renews within our hearts. Every generation has its own Temple. When a nation, an institution, and even a religious system is believed to be unshakable, yet collapse, the ancient fall of Jerusalem reminds us that God's presence is never confined to architecture. He dwells within the humble and contrite heart. (Isaiah 57: 15) Therefore, the lesson of 70 CE is eternal. When the temple falls, build an altar of faith. When the walls crack, raise songs of hope. For one day the stone will again sing.

Epilogue – Out of Ashes, Everlasting Hope

The Roman fires that consumed the Second Temple did not consume the promise of *Adonai*. The people survived, scripture endured, and from a cross outside those walls rose a Kingdom no flame in touch. History closed one chapter to begin another. The advent of the age of word and spirit among the nations.

After two millennia, the mount once blackened by fire still grows with prayer. Pilgrims whisper ancient words and wait for the same Lord who promised to return in glory. The watchword remains, "Comfort, comfort My people says your God. Tell Jerusalem her warfare has ended." (Isaiah 40: 1- 2) The temple fell, but faith rose. And the story of Israel, and all those who call upon the God of Israel, continues marching toward a Jerusalem whose light will never again fail.

12

Faith Without a Temple
Rebuilding the Spirit

When the embers of Jerusalem's war cooled in 70 CE, the world of Israel seemed to have ended. The House of *Adonai* lay in ruins, priests had scattered or perished, and Levitical choirs no longer sang the Psalms of ascent. Smoke darkened Judea's sky, and despair hung like morning fog across the hills. Yet even in silence, prophecy breathed, "Though the fig tree does not bud and there are no grapes on the vines. . . . Yet I will rejoice in *Adonai*, I will exult in the God of my salvation." (Habakkuk 3:17-18)

From that posture of ruin rose one of history's greatest acts of spiritual resilience. With temple sacrifice gone, Israel rediscovered worship in study, prayer, and community. Out of loss came reinvention, and once again, out of exile came enduring faith. This chapter traces that rebirth. From the council of *Yavneh* that shaped post temple Judaism to the scattered followers of Messiah who learned to serve God amid gentile nations, and until finally both streams faced the tragedy of *Bar Kokhba's* revolt.

Yavneh – The School That Saved *Torah*

Rabbinic tradition tells that during Jerusalem's fall pharisaic sages *Yohanan Ben Zakai* escaped the city in a coffin, carried by disciples to Roman lines. He requested an audience with Vespasian, predicting his rise to emperor. When the prophecy came true, Vespasian granted him one petition. He requested, "Give me *Yavneh* and its sages."

That modest request saved Judaism. In a coastal town West of Jerusalem, *Yohanan Ben Zakai* established an Academy a new Sanhedrin without altar or king, where scholars could reweave the fabric of Israel's faith.[105] The first decision of Yavneh's council was theological triage. It diagnosed the issue of how to obey *Torah* without the Temple. Three pillars emerged:

1. *Tefillah* (prayer) in place of sacrifice, based on Hosea 14:3, "We will offer the bulls of our lips."

2. *Torah* study as daily worship. Reading Scripture became service equal to incense.

3. Acts of compassion (*tzedakah* and *chesed*) as practical holiness.

Rabban Yochanan taught, "Since the Temple was destroyed, the world stands on three things: *Torah*, worship, and deeds of loving-kindness." (Later echoed in Pirkei Avot 1:2) Thus, holiness survived the loss of geography.[106]

At Yavneh, the sages standardized the *Amidah* (standing prayer). This standing prayer consisted of Eighteen blessings to be prayed while facing Jerusalem. The ritual replaced the priests daily offering with the worshipper's continual heart. New liturgical lines

---

¹⁰⁵ *Babylonian Talmud*, Gittin 56a–b.
¹⁰⁶ Mishnah, *Pirkei Avot* 1:2; *Babylonian Talmud*, Berakhot 26b; Sukkah 49b.

mourned the Temple's fall, "Restore your presence to Zion . . . Rebuild Jerusalem speedily and in our days." The prayer book (*Siddur*) we use centuries later still carries that yearning.[107]

Without sacrifice, the rabbis, or Israel's teachers, became spiritual successors of the priest. Instruction was new meditation. Every Jewish village soon had a synagogue and *beit midrash* (house of study). Family tables became altars and Sabbath candles replaced temple lamps.[108]

Yavneh's assembly discussed which writings belonged to scripture. The five books of Moses were undisputed. The Prophets and Psalms long cherished were also included. However, debate centered on the inclusion of Ecclesiastes, Esther, and Song of Songs. In the end, they affirmed them all, declaring that every word breathed of holiness.[109] By the close of the 2nd century, Rabbi *Akiva* would teach, "Even the least letter is a mountain of law." [110] Canonization anchored identity for generations of exile to come.

Pilgrim feasts, once tied to Jerusalem, became diaspora memories. At Passover, Jews now asked at the table, "Why is this night different?" since they no longer brought lamb to the altar but recounted the deliverance through story. *Sukkot*, without temple processions, moved to rooftop

---

[107] *Babylonian Talmud*, Berakhot 28b–30a; Ismar Elbogen, *Jewish Liturgy: A Comprehensive History* (Philadelphia: Jewish Publication Society, 1993), 23–30.

[108] Cohen, Shaye J. D. *From the Maccabees to the Mishnah*, 3rd ed. (Louisville: Westminster John Knox, 2014), 219–223.

[109] Mishnah, *Yadayim* 3:5; *Babylonian Talmud*, Megillah 7a; Shaye J. D. Cohen, 227–229.

[110] *Babylonian Talmud*, Menachot 29b.

booths worldwide. Even mourning became prayer, each year's *Tisha b'Av* fast memorialized both temple destructions, turning national tragedy into discipline of remembrance.[111]

Preserving Faith in Exile

Believers in *Yeshua* were mostly Jewish during these decades. They understood the Temple's fall as both judgments predicted by their master and vindication of his promise that God would dwell within his followers in the diaspora. Syria, Asia Minor, Egypt, and beyond formed synagogue-like congregations (*ekklesiai*) devoted to Scripture reading, prayer, and breaking bread. The book of Hebrews, likely written soon after 70 CE, interpreted the destruction as heavenly transition, "We have an altar from which those serving the Tabernacle have no right to eat." (Hebrews 13:10) "We have a Kingdom that cannot be shaken." (Hebrews 12:28) Through these words, faith pivoted from place to Person to people.[112]

Initially Messianic Jews remained in synagogues, sharing prayers and Scripture but diverging on the identity of Messiah. Tensions grew as gentile believers increased and Rome watched for sedition. *Yavneh's* sages added the *Birkat ha-Minim* (Blessings against Heretics) to the *Amidah* which was likely aimed at the groups dividing their communities. Messianic Jews found themselves quietly excluded from worship their ancestors had

---

[111] Mishnah, *Pesachim* 10:4; *Ta'anit* 4:6; Shaye J. D. Cohen, 223–227.
[112] Dunn, James D. G. *The Partings of the Ways* (London: SCM Press, 2006), 71–79; Harold W. Attridge, *The Epistle to the Hebrews* (Philadelphia: Fortress Press, 1989), 393–399.

formed. [113] Painful as it was, this separation forced elucidative definitions. The followers of *Yeshua* had to clarify faith apart from the Temple or National Center while still rooted in Israel's scriptures.

Life under Rome: Administration and Taxes

After the war, Rome imposed the Fiscus Judaicus, a tax of two denarii each year payable to the Capitoline Temple in Rome. This was the very temple of Jupiter that mocked their God. Payment was humiliation, but non-payment meant death. Persecution was social as much as political, and Jews became suspect citizens across the empire.[114]

Governors stationed at Caesarea supervised a land whose spirit they never understood. The Tenth Legion (Fretensis) camped on the temple mount, their pig-symbol standard served as an ongoing affront. Jerusalem was slowly transformed into a Roman outpost.[115]

Yet faith outlasted occupation. Synagogues rose in Sepphoris, Tiberius, and Capernaum. Galilee replaced Jerusalem as the heart of *Torah* study. From these schools would emerge the great rabbis of *Mishnah*.

Born shortly before the temple destruction, *Akiva Ben Yosef* rose from shepherd to preeminent teacher. He interpreted scripture with creative precision, often finding

---

[113] *Babylonian Talmud*, Berakhot 28b–29a; James D. G. Dunn, 222–230.
[114] Suetonius, *The Twelve Caesars*, trans. Robert Graves (London: Penguin Classics, 2007), 311–313; Cassius Dio, *Roman History*, trans. Earnest Cary (Cambridge: Harvard University Press, Loeb), 8:283–285.
[115] Flavius Josephus, *The Jewish War*, trans. G. A. Williamson, 399–402; Fergus Millar, *The Roman Near East* (Cambridge: Harvard University Press, 1993), 70–74.

meaning in individual letters. "Every crown on the *Torah* has mountains of law."[116]

He taught that even Rome served God's plan, "All that he does is for God." His disciples compiled oral tradition that later formed *Mishna* the foundation of *Talmud*. Akiba's generation also faced a new uprising and he like others mistook its leaders for the Messiah.[117]

Sixty years after Jerusalem's fall, emperor Hadrian visited Judea. At first, he permitted the rebuilding of the city, then announced it would be a Roman colony to be named Aelia Capitalina, with a temple to Jupiter on the temple Mount. Outrage erupted and into this flashpoint rose *Shimon bar Kosiba*, a brilliant commander. Rabbi Akiba hailed him as *Bar Kokhba*, "Son of the Star," from Numbers 24:17, "A star will come out of Jacob." Many believed Messiah had arrived.

For two years Jewish forces won astonishing victories. Coins were minted with Hebrew inscriptions "Year-one of the Redemption of Israel." Jerusalem was briefly recaptured. Sacrifices were offered again on Mount Zion. Joy swept every village and prayers of Psalm 126 sounded fulfilled. "When *Adonai* restored the captives of Zion, we were like dreamers."[118]

Hadrian sent General Julius Severus and twelve legions, over 120 thousand soldiers, to reclaim the Judean hills systematically. By 135 CE the revolt was crushed. Fifty fortified cities and 985 villages were destroyed. Hundreds

---

[116] *Babylonian Talmud, Menachot* 29b; Shaye J. D. Cohen, 232–236.
[117] Jerusalem *Talmud, Ta'anit* 4:5 (68d); Shaye J. D. Cohen, 236–245.
[118] Dio, Cassius. *Roman History*, trans. Earnest Cary (Cambridge: Harvard University Press, Loeb), 8:449–457; Jerusalem *Talmud, Ta'anit* 4:5 (68d).

of thousands were killed, and many were enslaved. *Bar Kokhba* perished at Betar on the 9th of *Av*, again the same date as both Temples' falls. The repetition of calamity seemed to be heaven's sad signature.

Hadrian banned circumcision and *Torah* study, exiled Jews from Jerusalem, and rebuilt Aelia Capitolina with inscriptions prohibiting Jewish entry under pain of death. He renamed the province Syria Palestina to erase Israel's memory. A century after Herod, the land once pulsing with pilgrims lay silent again. From rabbinic Judaism this was the end of armed messianism. For Messianic believers, it confirmed that only the true son of David could bring a lasting Kingdom. Only Spirit, not zeal, would conquer empire.[119]

After 135 CE Jews were dispersed through Rome's expanses of North Africa, Babylonia, Spain, and Gaul. Babylonian Jews established academies at Sura and Pumbedita, which would centuries later compile the Babylonian *Talmud*. Faith became a portable nation bound by Sabbath instead of soil.

Believers in *Yeshua* spread along the same roots. Paul's earlier missions had prepared ground. Now his letters became scripture to the exiled communities. Synagogue readings and home gatherings continued side by side, showing shared heritage. Without temple or sovereignty, who were the people of God? The answer evolved differently in each branch:

- Rabbinic Judaism defined Israel through *Torah* obedience and study—a scroll-bound people.

---

[119] Dio, Cassius. 163–166.

- Messianic Judaism / Early Christianity defined Israel through the Spirit and faith in Messiah—a Spirit bound people.

Yet both kept alive the core truths that creation is good, law is holy, and God's promises are irrevocable. The apostle Paul's word written three decades before 70 CE, rang prophetic, "Did God reject his people? May it never be! For I also am an Israelite." (Romans 11:1)[120]

Caught teaching *Torah* after Hadrian's ban, *Akiva* was flayed alive. During execution, his lips reciting the *Sh'ma* as he died, "Hear O Israel, *Adonai* is our God, *Adonai* is one." The *Talmud* says he smiled, explaining, "All my life I waited to love him with all my soul." His death embodied the heart of Deuteronomy 6:5.[121]

Believers also faced sporadic persecution under emperors Domitian and Trajan. They refused to offer incense to Caesar but prayed for him. That attitude was born from Jeremiah 29:27, "Seek the *Shalom* of the city to which I have carried you."[122] Their martyrdoms did for the Gospel what *Akiva's* did for *Torah*. They proved faith's worth greater than life.

Both streams of believers shared psalms of comfort amid exile, "By the rivers of Babylon, there we sat and wept when we remembered Zion." (Psalm 137:1) Yet they also sang, "Those who sow in tears will reap with songs of joy." (Psalm 126:5)

---

[120] James D. G. Dunn, 70–79, 239–246; N. T. Wright, *Paul and the Faithfulness of God* , 1230–1240.

[121] *Babylonian Talmud*, Berakhot 61b.

[122] Pliny the Younger, *Letters*, trans. Betty Radice (London: Penguin Classics, 1969), 287–293; Eusebius, *Ecclesiastical History*, trans. G. A. Williamson (London: Penguin Classics, 1989), 132–138.

Faith without a Temple was not faith without God. He had moved his dwelling from gold to hearts. The Western Wall's stones remained silent witnesses, but across empires new sanctuaries of spirit rose behind wandering eyes. Theological consequences erupted from this era:

1. Atonement Re-imagined. With no altar for blood, atonement shifted towards ethical living including repentance (*teshuvah*), prayer and charity made expiation.

2. Universal Access to God. Jews discovered that holiness could flourish in diaspora. Believers in *Yeshua* saw gentiles enter covenant without pilgrimage to Zion. From different roots, both reached the conviction that God is present when his name is remembered.

3. Scripture as Sanctuary. Scroll and spirit became the new mercy seat. Study was worship and obedience became sacrifice. The *Torah* and the gospel both insisted that hearing must be followed by doing.

Parallels of Persistence

By the 2nd century's close, both Judaism and Christianity were codifying heritage. The *Mishna* set in writing the oral law (around ~200 CE). Messianic communities gathered the gospels and Apostolic letters into Canon. History's trajectory moved from independent movements to world religions, yet each carried the memory of a shared temple and a covenant God who dwells with his people.

The collapse of Jerusalem once seemed the silencing of heaven. Instead, it became the birth of a faith architecture that no army can touch.

- Where bricks fell, books rose.
- Where priests died, teachers began.
- Where pilgrimage ceased, prayer spread.
- Where altar ashes blew, Spirit fire descended.

For believers today, their story asks, how do we worship when structures crumble? How do we build faith in exile? Their answer was by turning homes into sanctuaries, study into praise, and hope into daily work. When faith moves from place to person, from tradition to transformation, the temple never ceases. Rather, it multiplies.

Epilogue – Ashes and Promise

From 70 to 135 CE the world learned again that *Adonai*'s presence cannot be burned or banished. Empires erase names, but God writes them on palms. Even Hadrian's edicts could not quench Isaiah's assurance, "Comfort, comfort my people . . . The glory of *Adonai* will be revealed, and all flesh will see it together." (Isaiah 40:1, 5)

Faith without a temple motivated an expansion of a movement from shadow to substance, from gold to spirit, and from mountains to hearts of flesh. The story never collapsed but continued. And so, history awaits its final chapter when the voices of both Israel and the nations will sing together, "Behold the dwelling of God is with men." (Revelation 21:3)

Part V: The Temple that Lives On

13

From Ruins to Renewal
Jewish Faith after 70 CE

The altar was gone, the priests were scattered, and the songs of ascent ceased from Mount Zion. Yet even as smoke rose from the ruins, words began to rise in its place. The prophets had already given language for such disaster. Lamentations, once written for the Babylonian destruction, found new life on Jewish lips, "Is it nothing to you, all you who pass by? Look and see if there is any pain like my pain, which was dealt out to me." (Lamentations 1:12) Three strands of mourning formed and then shaped post-Temple Jewish prayer:

- Daily remembrance of Zion. Blessings in the *Amidah* petitioned, "Return in mercy to Jerusalem Your city and dwell in it as You have promised. Rebuild it soon in our days." This made longing for Jerusalem a daily discipline, not a once-a-year grief.

- *Tisha b'Av* as a liturgical anchor. The ninth of *Av* became the yearly fast of destruction, weaving together memory of the devastations of both the First and Second Temples. On that day, congregations sat on the floor, chanted Lamentations by candlelight, and recited *kinnot* (elegies) that recast recent horrors through biblical lament. Mourning was not suppressed. Rather, it was given a structure, a voice, and a hope.

- Wedding joy mixed with sorrow. Even at a wedding, in the height of celebration, a glass is shattered under the *chuppah* to recall Jerusalem's fall. The *Talmud* preserves the instinct behind this. [123] When rabbis saw a house overly decorated, they ordered a corner left unfinished "in remembrance of the Temple." [124]

Every joy kept a place for longing, fulfilling the psalmist's vow, "If I forget you, O Jerusalem, let my right hand forget her skill." (Psalm 137:5)

This liturgical mourning did more than look backward. It taught each generation that grief, held before God, can become a wellspring of hope. Tears turned into a form of covenant loyalty. To remember the ruins, was to trust that God still had a future for His people.

Synagogue, study, and the Presence of God

With the Temple destroyed, a new question pressed urgently, where could Israel now meet God? Without sacrifices, priests, or pilgrim feasts, what would covenant life look like?

Rabbinic teachers answered not with new stones but with new structures of time and community. *Yavneh's* sages gathered soon after 70 CE and began to reorder worship around the three pillars of synagogue prayer, *Torah* study, and deeds of loving-kindness. "For My House

---

[123] *Babylonian Talmud*, Berakhot 30b–31a.
[124] *Babylonian Talmud*, Bava Batra 60b.

will be called a House of Prayer for all nations."
(Isaiah 56:7)[125]

That verse, once applied to the Temple, now re-echoed in synagogues from Galilee to Babylonia. Every local congregation where ten Jews gathered to pray was taught that the *Shekhinah*, the Divine Presence, dwelt with them. (Pirkei Avot 3:6) *Mishnah Avot* would eventually affirm that when ten sit and study *Torah* together, the Presence rests with them. Even two studying, or one reading alone, are not without His nearness. (Mishnah Avot 3:6) Two profound shifts defined this renewal:

- The synagogue as micro-Temple. The *aron kodesh* (holy ark) that holds the *Torah* scroll became a symbolic Ark of the Covenant. The *bimah*, where Scripture is read, echoed the Temple platform from which priests once proclaimed blessing. Instead of incense and offerings, there were psalms and blessings. Yet worshipers believed the same God listened. Morning and evening services mirrored the daily *tamid* offerings, so that lips became the new altar, "We will offer the bulls of our lips." (Hosea 14:3)

- The *beit midrash* (house of study) as meeting place with God. Study of *Torah* and later *Mishnah* and *Talmud* was not mere education. Rather, it was encounter. Argument "for the sake of Heaven" was itself a form of worship. A page of *Talmud*, with *Mishnah* surrounded by generations of commentary,

---

[125] Mishnah, *Pirkei Avot* 1:2; *Babylonian Talmud*, Berakhot 26b; Cohen, Shaye J. D. 219–223.

visually expressed the conviction that God's voice continued to echo through the ages. Psalm 1's promise, "His delight is in the *Torah* of *Adonai*, and on His *Torah*, he meditates day and night" (Psalm 1:2) became the blueprint of daily life.[126]

In this way, Jewish faith moved from a single sacred mountain to countless sacred tables where Scripture was opened. The Presence that once dwelt behind a veil in Jerusalem now accompanied exiles in Babylonia, Alexandria, Rome, and beyond.

Rabban Yohanan ben Zakkai is remembered as saying that since the Temple's fall, acts of mercy and study stand in place of sacrifice. The prophet's words proved true in new form, "He has told you, mankind, what is good, and what *Adonai* is seeking from you: to do justice, to love mercy, and to walk humbly with your God." (Micah 6:8)[127]

Through mourning liturgies, synagogue worship, and the elevation of study, Jewish faith after 70 CE did not merely survive. In its place, it discovered that God's dwelling could never again be limited to stone. The ruins of the Temple became the foundation of a new sanctuary built in time, text, and community. The Presence walks with His people wherever they are scattered.

Reflection: Grief as Covenant Faithfulness

The fall of the Second Temple could easily have been the end of Israel's story, a final severing of land, altar, and

---

[126] *Babylonian Talmud*, Megillah 29a; Berakhot 6a, 26b; Mishnah, *Pirkei Avot* 3:2, 3:6; Ismar Elbogen, 31–40.
[127] *Avot de-Rabbi Natan*, 27–30.

people. Yet out of that shattering a paradox of grief becoming an act of covenant faithfulness. The practices like the daily remembrance of Zion, the fast of *Tisha b'Av*, and the deliberate mingling of joy with sorrow at weddings train the heart to refuse both denial and despair. To remember the ruins is to insist that history is still held within God's promises, even when the visible signs of those promises lie in ashes.

This is not nostalgia for a lost golden age. It is a liturgy of protest and hope. When a bride and groom hear the crack of glass beneath the *chuppah*, joy is not diminished so much as deepened. The moment silently declares that no individual happiness can be complete while the world, and Jerusalem, remain unhealed. In that sense, every Jewish home begins under the sign of incompleteness. The brokenness is not hidden away. Rather, it is named, carried, and embodied as a commentary on Psalm 137's vow not to forget Zion.

This period motivated a profound move from "where" to "how." When the physical Temple fell, the immediate question was spatial, where can we now meet God? The rabbinic response addressed the question of how to live in a way that invites His Presence into our lives. Synagogue prayer, acts of mercy, and the *beit midrash* re-inscribed sacred space into sacred time and sacred relationships. The altar migrated from stone to speech, from Jerusalem's courts to the human mouth that prays and the heart that wrestles with Torah.

There is a quiet boldness in declaring that when ten gather to pray, or when two argue a point of *halakhah* "for the sake of Heaven," the *Shekhinah* dwells among them. It means exile is never purely exile. The Presence that once concentrated behind a veil now diffuses through the people's shared study and mutual kindness.

What emerges, then, is not a faith that has learned to "make do" without a Temple, but a faith that has discovered deeper layers of the same God. The sacrificial system had always pointed beyond itself to justice, mercy, and humility before God, as the prophets insisted. After 70 CE, those prophetic accents became the standard to feed the hungry, to welcome the stranger, and to seek peace in community. The ethical life becomes liturgy extended into the home and on the street. A visit to the sick or a coin slipped quietly into a poor hand is a kind of offering, placed on the hidden altar of the heart.

This shift does not erase loss. Although priests are scattered, songs are silenced, and pilgrims no longer converge on Zion during feasts, Jewish practices refused to let loss be the final word. The same writings that lament destruction also imagine restoration. The synagogue's ark, holding the Torah scroll, does not pretend to be the Ark of the Covenant, yet it gestures toward it. The *bimah* is not the Temple court, yet it echoes the memory of priests blessing the people. Every echo keeps the original sound alive. In this way, post-Temple Judaism lives in a creative tension of being fully present in its new forms, yet never forgetting the older music it still waits to hear again.

Epilogue: A Sanctuary Without Walls

Imagine a small synagogue in a Galilean village, perhaps a generation after the destruction. The elders still remember the last pilgrimage they made to Jerusalem as children. The younger ones have only heard about it in stories. On a summer evening, lamps are lit, and the congregation gathers. There is no altar here, no smoke rising into the sky, and no priestly trumpets to announce the beginning of worship. Yet the people rise as the ark is opened. A scroll is carried through the room, and they reach out, not to touch the parchment itself, but to draw near to the words that have carried them this far.

A boy chants from the prophets, his voice trembling. An old woman in the corner mouths the verses, tears streaming down her face. Somewhere in the liturgy, prayers for Jerusalem's rebuilding are offered, their words smooth yet not rote. Each repetition is a stone laid in a house only God can finish.

Later that week, worshipers gather around a worn table with *Mishnah* or *midrash*. They argue fiercely, laugh, and bless each other. Voices rise, hands wave, and someone remarks, half joking, that the *Shekhinah* smiles at their search for truth. In the heat of debate, they believe Heaven listens.

At home, a couple prepares for their daughter's wedding. The house is decorated, but one corner remains bare. Under the wedding canopy, as blessings are spoken and joy swells, the groom will bring his foot down to shatter a glass. For a moment, everyone is stilled as they remember that the Temple, the city, and their people have endured. Then the shout goes up, "*Mazal tov!*" and dancing begins.

In the world created by ruins of 70 CE, the Presence dwells now in the cadence of Hebrew prayers spoken in exile, in acts of mercy done quietly in crowded streets, and in the rustle of pages turning late at night as students trace the arguments of sages long gone. The loss of the Temple remains a wound, but it has also become a doorway. Through it, Israel learned again that the God who chose Zion is the same God who walks with His people on unmarked roads.

From ruins to renewal, from stone to scroll, from a single sanctuary to a scattered people who carry the sanctuary within them, this is not the end of the story. Rather it is its unfolding. If the words are spoken, the songs are remembered, and the debates continue, then the shattered glass beneath the *chuppah* will not only recall what was destroyed. It will also shine with the promise of what will yet be restored.

14

Early Disciples
The Temple and Disciples of *Yeshua*

The earliest Messianic community was born in the shadow of Herod's Temple. *Yeshua*'s disciples were Galilean Jews who had grown up making pilgrimage to Jerusalem for the feasts, offering sacrifices, and reciting psalms of ascent as they climbed the hill of *Adonai*. Even after His death and resurrection, they did not abandon that rhythm.

The book of Acts describes them this way, "Day by day, they continued with one mind, spending time at the Temple and breaking bread from house to house. They were sharing meals with gladness and sincerity of heart, praising God and having favor with all the people." (Acts 2:46-47) Two centers of worship operated side by side:

- The Temple courts. Peter and John went up at the hour of prayer, healed a lame man at the Beautiful Gate, and preached under Solomon's Portico. They were still participating in the daily services, likely reciting the *Amidah* and the *Shema* with their fellow Jews.

- The home gatherings. In homes they broke bread "in remembrance" of *Yeshua*'s death and resurrection, interpreting the Passover symbols through Him. What had been a single annual festival now overflowed into weekly, even daily, table-fellowship that remembered the Lamb who was slain.

For a time, they lived in the tension of being fully within the stream of Second Temple Judaism yet convinced that *Yeshua* was the long-promised Messiah who had transformed the meaning of sacrifice and presence.

Yeshua's prophecies and the looming crisis

Yeshua had spoken words that hovered over the community like storm clouds, "Do you see all these things? Amen, I tell you, not one stone will be left here upon another, which will not be torn down." (Matthew 24:2) "Jerusalem, Jerusalem, who kills the prophets and stones those sent to her! . . . Behold, your house is left to you desolate!" (Matthew 23:37-38)

He had wept over the city, warning of encircling armies and utter devastation. When the revolt against Rome erupted in 66 CE and Roman legions closed in, those prophecies were remembered with new urgency. Early sources and later church historians preserve the tradition that many believers of *Yeshua* in Jerusalem heeded His warning, "When you see Jerusalem surrounded by armies, then recognize that her devastation is near" (Luke 21:20) and fled across the Jordan to Pella. Whether every detail can be confirmed or not, it is clear that the war scattered the Jerusalem community and forced them into a truly post-Temple existence.[128]

The letter to the Hebrews, likely composed in the years leading up to or just after 70 CE, reads like a pastoral word to believers who felt the ground of Temple-centered worship shaking beneath them. Its message presented the reality to which the Temple pointed has already come in Messiah. The loss of the building, while traumatic, does not mean the loss of access to God. "Now when Messiah appeared as *Kohen Gadol* of the good things that have now come, passing through the greater and more perfect Tent not made with hands . . . He entered into the Holy of Holies once for all—not by the blood of goats and calves but by His own blood, having obtained eternal redemption." (Hebrews 9:11-12)

This was not abstract theology, but it was survival. When the Temple burned, believers clung to the conviction that they had a High Priest and sanctuary that no army could reach.

From the beginning of His ministry, *Yeshua* had spoken of the Temple in startlingly personal terms. After His first cleansing of the courts, when challenged for a sign, He answered, "Destroy this Temple, and in three days I will raise it up!" . . . But He was talking about the Temple of His body. (John 2:19, 21)

The Fourth Gospel explicitly interprets *Yeshua*'s body as the true Temple. In the agency of *Yeshua*, is the place where heaven and earth meet, and where God's glory dwells in

---

[128] Eusebius, 127–129; Wright, N. T. *Jesus and the Victory of God*, 339–347.

visible form. This image shapes much of the apostolic reflection that follows.

Incarnation as indwelling

John's prologue declares, "And the Word became flesh and tabernacled among us. We looked upon His glory, the glory of the one and only from the Father, full of grace and truth." (John 1:14) The verb "tabernacled" deliberately recalls the wilderness Tent of Meeting and, by extension, the Temple. In *Yeshua*, the *Shekhinah* Presence that once filled Solomon's house now fills a human life that was walking, speaking, healing, and forgiving.

Wherever He goes, whether in Galilean villages, synagogues, or in the courts of Herod's Temple, He behaves as if He Himself were the meeting place between God and Israel. As the special envoy and agent of God, He pronounces forgiveness apart from sacrifice (Mark 2:5), offers living water apart from the Temple's water-drawing ceremony (John 7:37-38), and declares Himself the light of the world in the very courts where great lamps burned during *Sukkot* (John 8:12). The New Covenant writings repeatedly map Temple imagery onto *Yeshua*'s death and resurrection:

- Passover lamb. John the Immerser announces Him, "Behold, the Lamb of God who takes away the sin of the world!" (John 1:29). Paul later writes, "Messiah, our Passover Lamb, has been sacrificed." (1 Corinthians 5:7)

- High Priest. Hebrews calls Him "a *Kohen Gadol* forever according to the order of Melchizedek."

(Hebrews 6:20; 7:17) He enters not the earthly Holy of Holies but the heavenly one, offering His own blood, and then sits at the right-hand of God, continually interceding. (Hebrews 7:25)

- Mercy Seat and atonement. Paul uses Temple language when he says God set forth *Yeshua* as a *hilastērion,* a mercy seat, through faith in His blood (Romans 3:25). In Him, the place of atonement is no longer a golden cover between cherubim but the crucified and risen Messiah Himself.

When the Gospels describe the veil of the Temple tearing from top to bottom now of His death (Matthew 27:51), they are proclaiming both judgment on the old order and the opening of direct access to God. The barrier is torn in Him, and the Holy of Holies has, in some sense, stepped out to meet the world.

The resurrection completes this image. The Temple-of-His-body is destroyed and then raised in three days, just as He promised. For believers, this meant that God had already built the indestructible sanctuary Ezekiel foresaw. A sanctuary not in stone, but in the living, glorified Messiah. "Therefore, since we have a great *Kohen Gadol* who has passed through the heavens, *Yeshua Ben-Elohim,* let us hold firmly to our confessed allegiance." (Hebrews 4:14)

Their worship no longer depended on the survival of any earthly shrine. The true Temple had ascended above the reach of siege and fire.

The most radical step in this unfolding revelation comes when the apostles begin to apply Temple language, not only to *Yeshua,* but to His people. The community of believers, both Jews and Gentiles grafted into the covenant, becomes the new dwelling of the Divine Presence. Peter writes to scattered believers in Asia Minor, "You also, as living stones, are being built up as a spiritual house—a holy priesthood, to offer up spiritual sacrifices acceptable to God through Messiah *Yeshua*." (1 Peter 2:5)

Here the *ekklēsia* is not a loose association but a Temple under construction. Each disciple is a stone, and together they form a house where priestly service, not with animal blood but with praise, obedience, and acts of mercy continues.

Paul uses similar language in Ephesians, "So then you are no longer strangers and foreigners, but you are fellow citizens with God's people and members of God's household. You have been built on the foundation made up of the emissaries and prophets, with Messiah *Yeshua* Himself being the cornerstone. In Him the whole building, being fitted together, is growing into a holy temple for the Lord. In Him, you also are being built together into God's dwelling place in the *Ruach*." (Ephesians 2:19-22) There are three key convictions from this era that emerge. The foundation is the apostolic and prophetic witness. The cornerstone is Messiah Himself, aligning and supporting all other stones. And the builder is the *Ruach HaKodesh*, shaping a living Temple that spans place and time.

This imagery dignified small, often persecuted gatherings with cosmic significance. A handful of believers meeting in a home in Corinth or Rome could see themselves as part of the same holy structure as the community in Jerusalem or Antioch.

The Spirit as *Shekhinah*

Paul presses the metaphor further, "Don't you know that you are God's temple and that the *Ruach Elohim* dwells among you?" (1 Corinthians 3:16) "What agreement does God's Temple have with idols? For we are the temple of the living God—just as God said, 'I will dwell in them and walk among them; I will be their God, and they shall be My people.'" (2 Corinthians 6:16)

Here "you" is plural and is the gathered community. The *Shekhinah* that once filled the Sanctuary now rests upon assemblies of believers. To divide, defile, or despise the community is to damage the Temple of God. To love, serve, and build it up is to honor the Presence. At the same time, Paul can speak in the singular, "Or don't you know that your body is a temple of the *Ruach ha-Kodesh* who is in you, whom you have from God, and that you are not your own?" (1 Corinthians 6:19)

The individual body becomes a small sanctuary, called to purity and holiness because God dwells within. The ethics of discipleship such as fleeing sexual immorality and pursuing love are grounded in this reality.

These statements did not emerge in a vacuum. As rabbinic Judaism emphasized that the *Shekhinah* rests upon ten gathered to pray or two studying *Torah*. Believers in *Yeshua* confessed a similar yet Christ-centered truth when dealing with discipline within a community, "Where two or three gather in His Name, He is in their midst." (Matthew 18:20)

Both communities, in different ways, were learning that God's dwelling had moved from one geographic point to communities shaped by His word and presence. For believers, the decisive difference was that the Messiah Himself had become the cornerstone and mediating High Priest.

Worship without walls: early practices

In the decades after 70 CE, Messianic communities across the empire adapted their worship in light of this Temple-as-Messiah-and-community vision. Acts and the later apostolic writings reveal four recurring elements:

1. Apostolic teaching (the Word). Readings from the *Torah* and Prophets, now joined to sayings and narratives about *Yeshua*, instructed and exhorted the community.

2. Fellowship (*koinonia*). Shared meals, mutual support, and care for the poor were treated as non-optional expressions of the new Temple's life.

3. Breaking of bread (the Table). The memorial meal originally rooted in Passover but celebrated regularly re-proclaimed *Yeshua*'s death until He comes (1 Corinthians 11:26). It was both sacrifice remembered and covenant renewed.

4. Prayers. Set prayers (often adapted from synagogue liturgy) and spontaneous intercession formed the incense of the new worship. Paul urges, "Pray without ceasing." (1 Thessalonians 5:17).

Together, these elements constituted a portable liturgy. A persecuted group in a catacomb in Rome or a small house in Philippi could enact the reality of the Temple without any physical altar. Messiah's sacrifice stood once for all, and the community's task was to live as His priesthood. [129] The apostolic writings reinterpreted "sacrifice" accordingly:

- Praise. "Through *Yeshua* then, let us continually offer up to God a sacrifice of praise—the fruit of lips giving thanks to His Name." (Hebrews 13:15).

- Doing good and sharing. "And do not neglect doing good and sharing, for with such sacrifices God is well pleased." (Hebrews 13:16).

- Lives of obedient love. Paul urges believers to present their bodies as a "living sacrifice, holy, acceptable to God" (Romans 12:1).

In each case, Temple language is retained but applied to a way of life rather than to ritual slaughter. The community becomes both altar and offering.

Finally, the apostolic vision looks beyond both the ruined Temple and the present community to the ultimate fulfillment. Revelation, written in the language of priestly and prophetic symbolism, envisions a New Jerusalem. "I saw no temple in her, for its Temple is *Adonai Elohei-Tzva'ot* and the Lamb." (Revelation 21:22)

Here the trajectory reaches its end, from Tabernacle to Temple, from Temple to Messiah, from Messiah to community, and from community to a renewed creation where God Himself and the Lamb are the Temple. There is

---

[129] Acts 2:42–47; 1 Corinthians 11:23–26; Wright, N. T. *Paul and the Faithfulness of God*, 1245–1255.

no longer need for a distinct sacred building because all reality has become sacred space.

Yet the imagery of priests and worship does not vanish, "They will be priests of God and of the Messiah, and they shall reign with Him for a thousand years." (Revelation 20:6) Believers' identity as a royal priesthood (1 Peter 2:9) continues into the age to come. The community, formed in history as a living Temple, will eternally serve in the unmediated Presence.

Reflection: living as Temple people

For the followers of *Yeshua*, the destruction of the Second Temple was not the end of God's dwelling with His people. Instead, it was the painful unveiling of a deeper reality already given in Messiah. They learned to see:

- In *Yeshua's* body, the true Temple. The meeting place of God and humanity, sacrifice and mercy, and priesthood and presence.
- In their gathered community, a holy building of living stones where the Spirit dwells.
- In their individual lives, small sanctuaries called to holiness in thought, body, and deed.

The stones of Jerusalem fell, but the Temple of Messiah and His people stand and grow. Wherever a small group gathers to open Scripture, break bread, and call on His Name, the promise is fulfilled again, "But two who are sitting together and there are words of Torah between them, the Divine Presence (*Shekhinah*) rests with them." (*Mishnah Avot* 3:2–3) To belong to Him is to be part of that Temple. A living, breathing dwelling of God in the Spirit, awaiting the day when the Lamb Himself will be its everlasting light.

15

A Vision of Restoration
The Future Hope

From the moment the first Temple fell, the God of Israel refused to let judgment have the last word. The prophets spoke into rubble with words that sounded almost impossible. Cities rebuilt, exiles regathered, hearts renewed, and a Jerusalem more glorious than anything Solomon had ever known are prophesied in the ultimate redemption.

Isaiah – comfort and a city of light

When Jerusalem lay threatened by Assyria and later crushed by Babylon, Isaiah was given a double burden. He was to announce judgment and then to sing comfort. "Comfort, comfort My people, says your God. Speak kindly to the heart of Jerusalem, and proclaim to her that her warfare has ended, that her iniquity has been removed—for she has received from *Adonai*'s hand double for all her sins." (Isaiah 40:1-2)

From chapter 40 onward, Isaiah presents a sweeping vision of restoration. Zion will be a place where the glory of *Adonai* rises like dawn, "Arise, shine, for your light has come! The glory of *Adonai* has risen on you." (Isaiah 60:1)

Nations stream not to exploit her but to learn from her, "Nations will come to your light, kings to the brilliance of your rising." (Isaiah 60:3) Jerusalem becomes the teaching center of the world. Swords are hammered into plowshares. War schools are closed forever (Isaiah 2:2-4). For a people scattered among hostile empires, this was not fantasy but covenant hope, that is anchored in God's unchanging promises to Abraham and David.

Jeremiah – a new covenant in the same land

Jeremiah watched Babylon's armies surround Jerusalem and saw the Temple burn, yet even as he purchased a field in a soon-to-be-ruined land, he heard this word, "Again fields and vineyards will be bought in this land." (Jeremiah 32:15) Beyond return to the soil, he foresaw a deeper restoration, "Behold, days are coming—it is a declaration of *Adonai*—when I will make a new covenant with the house of Israel and with the house of Judah . . . I will put My *Torah* within them. Yes, I will write it on their heart. I will be their God, and they will be My people." (Jeremiah 31:30-33)

The same God who once placed His Name in a house of stone would one day inscribe His ways in human hearts. The rebuilt Jerusalem of the future would not merely have walls and gates. Additionally, it would have a people transformed from within.

Ezekiel – from dry bones to a river of life

Ezekiel prophesied among exiles in Babylon who had lost Temple, land, and king. Into that despair came the vision of dry bones, "Behold, I will open your graves and make you come up out of your graves, My people. I will bring you back to the land of Israel." (Ezekiel 37:12)

He then saw a renewed Temple, a vast, measured sanctuary, and from its threshold a trickle of water flowing eastward (Ezekiel 40–47). As the stream deepened, it transformed the desert, even the Dead Sea became fresh, teeming with fish. "Every living creature that swarms will live wherever the rivers go. . . Their water flows from the Sanctuary." (Ezekiel 47: 9, 12)

Here the Temple is more than a building. It is the fountainhead of life for the whole world. The exiles, who once wept by the rivers of Babylon, were promised a day when a river from God's house would heal every river they knew.

Zechariah – the humble king and the holy city

Returning exiles under Zerubbabel and Joshua the high priest heard through Zechariah that their small, unimpressive second Temple was a seed of something greater. He foresaw a future king riding humbly on a donkey yet ruling from sea to sea (Zechariah 9:9-10), and a Jerusalem transformed. "Old men and old women will once again dwell in the streets of Jerusalem, each with his staff in hand because of great age. The streets of the city will be filled with boys and girls playing in its streets." (Zechariah 8:4-5)

Holiness would spread outward until even common pots were as sacred as Temple bowls (Zechariah 14:20-21). Instead of merely hosting worship, Jerusalem would embody it. Together, these prophets painted a multi-layered hope. This hope included a regathered people, a renewed land, a rebuilt Jerusalem, and a Temple whose influence extended to the ends of the earth. Their words left later generations watching history with one eye on headlines and the other on these promises.

The Temple as picture of God's eternal dwelling

By the time of *Yeshua* and the apostles, these prophetic hopes were part of Israel's spiritual vocabulary. Second Temple Jews prayed daily for the rebuilding of Jerusalem and the return of God's glory. Believers in *Yeshua* came to see that the restoration the prophets foretold unfolded in stages. These stages are manifested in Messiah Himself, in the Spirit-filled community, and finally in a renewed creation where God is all in all.

Messiah as firstfruits of restoration

Yeshua's resurrection was understood as the first piece of that promised future breaking into the present. Paul calls Him "the firstfruits of those who have fallen asleep" (1 Corinthians 15:20), an echo of the first sheaf once waved in the Temple at *Shavuot*. The prophets had promised resurrection (Isaiah 26:19; Daniel 12:2), and in Him that promise began to be fulfilled.

Likewise, the outpouring of the *Ruach* on *Shavuot* was interpreted as the arrival of the new covenant Jeremiah had promised. Peter quotes Joel, "I will pour out My *Ruach* on all flesh." (Joel 3:1 2:28; Acts 2:16-18) The new heart and Spirit Ezekiel foretold (Ezekiel 36:26-27) were given ahead of the final restoration, as a pledge that the rest of the promises would surely come. Early believers thus lived in a tension of an already but not yet reality.

- Already. The Messiah has come, died, risen, and poured out the Spirit. The new covenant has been inaugurated, and the Presence dwells in a living Temple made of people.

- Not yet. Death still reigns in bodies, injustice still scars nations, and Jerusalem still knows conflict. The full vision of Isaiah, Ezekiel, and Zechariah awaits completion.

Paul describes creation groaning like a woman in labor, waiting for the revealing of the sons of God (Romans 8:18-23). The future restoration is certain, but its full birth lies ahead. In this in-between time, the Temple's meaning expands even further. It becomes not only a memory of God's dwelling in the past but a picture of where history is going. Toward a world where God's presence is unmediated, universal, and joyous.

Hebrews draws explicitly on Temple imagery to point believers beyond the earthly sanctuary to a heavenly reality. "They offer service in a replica and shadow of the heavenly, one that is just as Moses was instructed by God when he was about to complete the Tabernacle ... But now *Yeshua* has obtained a more excellent ministry . . . He is Mediator of a better covenant." (Hebrews 8:5-6)

The earthly Tabernacle and Temple were never ends in themselves. Instead, they were shadows, sketches of the true dwelling of God. *Yeshua*, as High Priest in that heavenly sanctuary, guarantees that one day the distance between heaven and earth will be closed forever.

Nowhere is the future hope more fully portrayed than in the Revelation given to John. Exiled on Patmos, far from Jerusalem, he is granted a vision that gathers up the entire story of the Bible from Eden to Exodus, from Temple to exile, from Messiah's cross to the final renewal. John writes,

"Then I saw a new heaven and a new earth, for the first heaven and the first earth had passed away . . . I also saw the holy city—New Jerusalem—coming down out of heaven from God, prepared as a bride adorned for her husband." (Revelation 21:1-2)

Notice the direction. The city comes down from heaven to earth. The final hope is not escape from creation but God's descent to dwell in it. This fulfills the ancient Tabernacle promise, "Let them make Me a Sanctuary, so that I may dwell among them." (Exodus 25:8)

Now the voice from the throne declares, "Behold, the dwelling of God is among men, and He shall tabernacle among them. They shall be His people, and God Himself shall be among them and be their God." (Revelation 21:3)

The Hebrew word behind "dwelling" and "tabernacle" echoes the *Shekhinah*. A localized Prescence that the Temple in Jerusalem symbolized has become universal reality.

The New Jerusalem is described in terms that answer the deepest wounds of history, "He shall wipe away every tear from their eyes, and death shall be no more. Nor shall there be mourning or crying or pain any longer, for the former things have passed away." (Revelation 21:4)

The curses of Genesis 3, the griefs of Lamentations, and the exile sorrows of Psalm 137 are all reversed. Later John adds, "There shall no longer be any curse. . . Night shall be no more, and they shall have no need for the light of a lamp or the light of the sun, for *Adonai* Elohim will shine on them." (Revelation 22:3, 5)

This is the ultimate answer to the priestly blessing, "*Adonai* make His face to shine on you and be gracious to you" (Numbers 6:25). In the New Jerusalem, His shining is constant and unbroken. John's description of the city is saturated with Temple imagery:

- It is shaped like a cube (Revelation 21:16), echoing the cubic dimensions of the Holy of Holies in Solomon's Temple (1 Kings 6:20). The entire city is now as holy as that innermost room once was.
- Its foundations are adorned with precious stones reminiscent of the high priest's breastplate (Revelation 21: 19-20; Exodus 28:17-20). The city itself wears the garments of priesthood.
- A great high wall with twelve gates bears the names of the twelve tribes of Israel, while the foundations carry the names of the twelve emissaries of the Lamb (Revelation 21:12-14). Israel and the apostolic community are forever inscribed in its architecture.

Then comes the most astonishing statement, "I saw no temple in her, for its Temple is *Adonai Elohei-Tzva'ot* and the Lamb." (Revelation 21:22)

In the end, the symbol gives way to the Reality. There is no longer need for a separate sacred building because the whole city is sanctuary and God Himself is its Temple. The Lamb, *Yeshua,* is eternally united with the Father in this role. He is the One whose body was once called "this Temple" and His Spirit now fills the entire new creation as its holy place.

Drawing directly from Ezekiel's vision, John sees, "The river of the water of life—bright as crystal, flowing from the throne of God and of the Lamb down the middle of the city's street. On either side of the river was a tree of life, bearing twelve kinds of fruit, yielding its fruit each month; and the leaves of the tree were for the healing of the nations." (Revelation 22:1-2)

Ezekiel's Temple River, which healed the Dead Sea, has become the river of the city-Temple. The Tree of Life lost in Eden has been transplanted into the heart of the New Jerusalem. The Temple, now understood as God and the Lamb, is the source of life, nourishment, and healing for all peoples.

The nations, once divided at Babel and so often at war against Zion, now walk by the city's light and bring their glory into it (Revelation 21:24, 26). The vision of Isaiah 2 and 60 has come to pass. The prophets and apostles did not describe this future simply to satisfy curiosity. Their visions were meant to shape how God's people live in the present.

Holiness as anticipation

Because the New Jerusalem is a city where righteousness dwells, believers are called to live now as citizens of that city. Peter exhorts, "Since all these things are to be destroyed in this way, what kind of people ought you to be—living in holiness and godliness, looking for and hastening the coming of the day of God." (2 Peter 3:11-12) The Temple's purity laws, once tied to physical space, become ethical summons. Now, our choices either align us with that future holiness or resist it.

Every gathering of God's people is a small rehearsal of the New Jerusalem's worship. When communities sing psalms, break bread, and cry "Holy, holy, holy," they join the song of heaven described in Revelation 4–5. The earthly congregation becomes an outpost of the coming Temple-city. Hebrews says, "You have come to Mount Zion—to the city of the living God, the heavenly Jerusalem . . . to *Yeshua*, the Mediator of a new covenant." (Hebrews 12:22-24) Even now, in prayer and praise, believers step into the reality they will one day see with unveiled faces.

For a people who have known exile, persecution, and the destruction of beloved sanctuaries, the vision of restoration sustains endurance. The fall of the Second Temple, the burning of synagogues, or the closing of churches cannot overturn the promise, "For here we have no lasting city, but we are seeking the one that is to come." (Hebrews 13:14)

In every generation, this hope has enabled Abraham's children, by blood and by faith, to rebuild after devastation. They know that ultimate security is not in any earthly stone but in the city whose architect and builder is God. (Hebrews 11:10)

The Temple has journeyed from tent to stone, from ruin to rebuilding, from Messiah's body to the Spirit-filled community, and finally to the New Jerusalem where God and the Lamb are the everlasting sanctuary. The prophets of Israel saw this in glimpses:

- A city radiant with divine light (Isaiah).
- A covenant engraved on hearts (Jeremiah).
- A river flowing from God's house healing the world (Ezekiel).

- A Zion filled with children's laughter and nations' worship (Zechariah).

The apostles saw its beginning in *Yeshua* and its consummation in Revelation's final chapters. For them, and for all who follow, the Temple is no longer only a memory of what once was, but a promise of what will be, "He who sits on the throne said, 'Behold, I am making all things new!' Then He said, 'Write, for these words are trustworthy and true.'" (Revelation 21:5)

To believe this is to walk already in the light of that coming city. To live as living stones of the eternal Temple, to let our homes and communities become early echoes of God's future dwelling, and to wait with longing not merely for a building restored, but for a world remade where God will dwell with His people forever.

Epilogue
The Enduring House of God

Across these pages the House of God has risen, fallen, and risen again in new forms—tent and stone, smoke and song, Messiah and community, present struggle and future glory. What began as a desert tabernacle has become a story stretching from Eden's garden to the New Jerusalem, from the fire on Sinai to the light of the Lamb. The journey traced four great movements:

- Presence given. *Adonai* chose to dwell with a people, not because He needed a house, but because they needed a place to meet Him. The *Mishkan* and both Temples taught Israel that the Holy One is near yet approached in reverence.

- Presence hidden. Sin, idolatry, injustice, and baseless hatred tore down what had been built. Babylon's flames, Rome's legions, and centuries of exile scattered stones and singers alike. Yet even in judgment, voices of the prophets refused to let despair have the last word, "I will be for them a *mikdash me'at*—a little sanctuary—in the countries where they have gone." (Ezekiel 11:16) Synagogue, study hall, and faithful homes became small Temples in dispersion.

- Presence made flesh. In the fullness of time, the Word became flesh and tabernacled among us (John 1:14). *Yeshua* of Nazareth walked the courts of Herod's Temple as its true Lord and meaning. In His death the veil tore, in His resurrection the living Temple stood forever, and in His ascension and the outpouring of the *Ruach*, the *Shekhinah* moved into human hearts and communities. Believers discovered that they themselves were now a holy priesthood and a spiritual house (1 Peter 2:5).

- Presence promised forever. The last pages of Scripture show not a ruined city but a radiant one, coming down from heaven, where a loud voice cries, "Behold, the dwelling of God is among men." (Revelation 21:3) There is no temple in that city, "for its Temple is *Adonai Elohei-Tzva'ot* and the Lamb." (Revelation 21:22) The story ends where it began. God walking with His people, but now with every tear wiped away and every wound healed.

For Israel, the Temple has remained a wound and a promise. For the Body of Messiah, it has become a lens through which to see the cross, the resurrection, the *ekklesia*, and the world to come. For both, it is a sign that the God of Abraham chooses not to remain distant, but to bind His Name, His honor, and His heart to a particular people and, through them, to all nations.

This book has followed that one thread. God's relentless desire to dwell with us. No failure, no empire, no destruction has overturned that desire. Every rebuilding after ruin, every synagogue raised, every congregation gathered, every whispered *Kaddish* and every sung doxology has been a fresh inscription of the same truth. "For *Adonai* has chosen Zion; He has desired it for His dwelling: 'This is My resting place forever. Here I dwell, for I have desired it.'" (Psalm 132:13-14)

Today, the House of God endures wherever His Presence is welcomed:

- in the prayers of Israel facing Jerusalem,
- in followers of *Yeshua* who present their bodies as living sacrifices,
- in communities that seek justice, love mercy, and walk humbly with their God, and
- in classrooms and study circles where Scripture is opened with trembling joy.

Stones may fall, sanctuaries may be seized or burned, and borders may shift. Yet the true House of God cannot be confiscated or destroyed, because it is ultimately God Himself with His people. It is the Messiah who bears our names before the Father, it is the Spirit who makes hearts His dwelling, and it is the promise that one day heaven and earth will be one Temple, luminous with the presence of the Holy One.

Until that day, every table where bread is broken with thanksgiving, every assembly where His Name is called, and every act of mercy offered in faith becomes a preview of the age to come. All exist as a small room in the great House that is still being built.

And so, the story continues, not only in ancient stones and sacred texts, but in the choices and worship of those who, in every generation, dare to believe the oldest promise of all. "I will make My dwelling among them and walk among them. I will be their God, and they shall be My people." (2 Corinthians 6:16)

The Temple has fallen and risen, changed form and meaning, but the desire of God remains. The House of God endures in Israel, in Messiah, in the Spirit, and in the world that is even now being prepared to become His eternal home.

Discussion Questions

Chapter 1 When the Fire Fell: The Destruction of
Solomon's Temple

1. How does the chapter's opening imagery of smoke,
    sound, and smell shape your emotional response to
    the destruction of the Temple? Which detail stands
    out most to you, and why?

2. The Temple is described as "the meeting place
    between heaven and earth." How does that
    description influence your understanding of what
    was lost on the ninth of Av?

3. In what ways does the chapter connect Babylonian
    military power with Israel's covenant
    unfaithfulness rather than treating the fall of
    Jerusalem as only a political event?

4. How do the quotations from Psalm 137 function
    within the narrative? What do they reveal about the
    inner life of the exiles as they process their loss?

5. The text poses the question, "Had God abandoned
    His dwelling place?" How would you answer this
    question using Jeremiah 16:11–13 and the chapter's
    interpretation of judgment and mercy?

6. The author writes that "the ashes of Jerusalem
    would become the soil for the renewal of faith."
    What forms might that renewal take, and what
    evidence for such renewal can you identify later in
    Israel's story?

7. How does the depiction of famine, slaughter, and
    deportation in "The Trauma of Exile" expand your

understanding of what "exile" meant beyond simply living in a foreign land?

8. The poor who remain in the land are tasked with tending vineyards and fields. How does this detail challenge or deepen your picture of who experienced exile and how?

9. If the Temple was the "heartbeat of Israel's worship," what practices or institutions do you think began to take on that role after its destruction, and why might that shift be theologically significant?

10. Where do you see parallels between the spiritual "sickness" described in this chapter and challenges faced by faith communities today? How might this narrative speak prophetically into contemporary contexts?

Chapter 2 Return and Rebuilding: Hope Restored in Jerusalem

1. How does the chapter contrast "politics and conquest" with "providence," and what does that contrast suggest about how we should read imperial history in light of Isaiah 45 and Ezra 1?

2. In what ways does portraying Cyrus as *Adonai*'s "anointed" challenge or expand your understanding of whom God can use as an instrument of mercy?

3. The decree of Cyrus is described as sounding like "the end of exile and the beginning of hope." What emotions and expectations do you imagine the first hearers experienced, and why?

4. How does the description of the journey home (language, upbringing in Babylon, 900-mile trek) complicate the idea that "going back" is simple or purely joyful?

5. When the returnees arrive to "silence," rubble, weeds, and jackals, what spiritual or psychological tensions does this scene create between memory of Zion and present reality?

6. Why do you think the chapter emphasizes that the people "pitched their tents among the ruins" and immediately "lifted their eyes toward heaven"? What does this reveal about faith in devastated places?

7. Before any construction begins, the leaders build an altar among the ruins. What does this priority teach about the relationship between worship and rebuilding after catastrophe?

8. How does the portrayal of Zerubbabel (Davidic heir) and *Yeshua*/Joshua (high priest) shape your sense of leadership in seasons of restoration? What balance of political and priestly roles do you see here?

9. The chapter repeatedly ties historical events to specific Scriptures (Isaiah 45, Ezra 1). How does this interweaving of text and narrative model a way of reading current events through Scripture today?

10. Where do you see parallels between the community's call to "rebuild the House of God" in ruins and the kinds of rebuilding tasks facing contemporary faith communities or your own life?

Chapter 3 A People of the Book: The Birth of Judaism

1. The chapter says the rebuilding of the Second Temple was a "visible symbol" that exile had ended, but that a "quieter revolution" was happening underneath. What was that quieter revolution, and why was it more important than the building itself?

2. The author writes that after exile, "never again would worship depend solely on altar or monarchy." What does this tell you about how Israel's understanding of worship changed?

3. The chapter notes that Judaism became "a faith sustained by Scripture, study, community, and daily practice." Which of these four do you think is most important for keeping a faith alive, and why?

4. The text mentions the rise of the synagogue, a defined canon of Hebrew Scriptures, and oral teaching traditions. How did these three things help turn Israel into *Am HaSefer*," the People of the Book?

5. Malachi describes the priest as a "messenger of *Adonai-Tzva'ot*" whose lips "guard knowledge." How does this description expand the role of a priest beyond offering sacrifices?

6. Scribes (*soferim*) are shown copying scrolls "with reverence," where each stroke is an act of worship. What does this suggest about how they viewed the *Torah* and their work?

7. The chapter says scribes wrestled with how to keep *Shabbat* under Persian rule, tithe without Levitical stores, and stay pure among Gentiles. How do

these examples show the beginning of what later became rabbinic interpretation and *halakhah*?

8. The *Torah* is called the "constitution" of Israel's renewed identity and the "true sovereign" in place of a king. In what ways can a sacred text function like a constitution for a community or nation?

9. The author describes the *Torah* as an "invisible boundary of holiness that no empire could erase." What do you think that means, and how might that idea have encouraged Jews living under foreign rule?

10. Public reading of *Torah* under Ezra and Nehemiah became a regular practice for "men, women and all who could understand." How might this kind of communal reading shape a people's shared beliefs and daily behavior?

Chapter 4 When Greece Came East: The Challenge of Hellenism

1. In what ways did Greek rule differ from earlier empires like Babylon and Persia in how they treated conquered peoples, especially the Jews?

2. The chapter says the Greeks wanted to "transform" rather than "destroy or displace." What does this mean, and why might that be more tempting or dangerous for a people of faith?

3. How did Greek art, architecture, philosophy, and the gymnasium make Hellenism attractive to many nations? Give at least two examples from the text.

4. The author describes a "subtle threat" in Greek culture: measuring truth by human wisdom instead of divine revelation. How might that conflict with Israel's belief in *Torah*?

5. The chapter calls the encounter with Greece "the defining test of the Second Temple era." What made this period such a major test for the people of Israel?

6. How does the legend of Alexander bowing before the High Priest Jaddua show the theme of God's providence in history, according to the author?

7. Alexander allowed the Jews to keep their laws and temple worship. In your view, why does the author still say his "true legacy" was language rather than tolerance?

8. *Koine* Greek became a common language across the empire. How did this shared language create new opportunities for spreading Jewish and later Christian ideas?

9. The chapter compares *Koine* Greek to the time "since Babel." What is the significance of this comparison, and what does it suggest about the spiritual meaning of a shared language?

10. Judea ended up between the Ptolemies in Egypt and other Greek kingdoms after Alexander's death. How might this political position have added pressure to the question, "Can *Torah*-faith survive amid the glitter of Athens?"

Chapter 5 War for the Holy Place: The Maccabees and Hanukkah

1. The chapter says no generation is "born into peace by accident." What does this mean, and how does the story of the Maccabees show this idea in action?

2. How did the rule of the Seleucid kings weaken Judea and "squeeze" the covenant "between taxation and temptation"? Give at least two examples from the text.

3. Why did Antiochus IV Epiphanes demand religious uniformity, and how did his policies attack the core practices of Jewish faith?

4. Which of Antiochus's decrees do you think would have been the hardest for faithful Jews to obey, and why?

5. The chapter calls the defilement of the Temple an "abomination of desolation," echoing Daniel 11:31. How would this event have felt to Jews who believed the Temple was the center of God's presence?

6. The author says the people now faced something worse than exile— "erasure." What is the difference between exile and erasure, and why is erasure more frightening in this context?

7. How does Mattathias' speech in Modiin show his understanding of covenant loyalty, even when most nations were obeying the king?

8. Mattathias responds with violent resistance, killing both the officer and the apostate Jew. What ethical or theological questions does this raise for you about defending faith under persecution?

9. Why do you think Mattathias' call, "All who are zealous for *Torah* and maintain the covenant—

follow me!" was powerful enough to start a movement?

10. The author writes, "The flame of resistance was lit." In what ways can religious resistance be both spiritually inspiring and politically risky? Use examples from the chapter to support your answer.

Chapter 6 Kings and Priests: The Hasmonean Experiment

1. The chapter opens by asking, "Should priests become princes?" What concerns about mixing religious and political power does this question raise?

2. In ancient Israel, why were the roles of priest and king kept separate, and how did that separation help protect "spiritual integrity"?

3. What conditions—like the vacant throne of David and "silent" prophecy—pushed the Hasmonean priestly family to take on both priestly and royal roles?

4. The text says the Hasmonean experiment grew "out of necessity—and divine mystery." What might that phrase suggest about how the people viewed this change in leadership?

5. Why is the people's statement that Simon would rule "until a trustworthy prophet shall arise" described as "astonishing"? What does it reveal about their hopes and doubts?

6. The chapter notes that "the spirit of prophecy had been quiet since Malachi." How might living without active prophets shape the spiritual and political choices of the community?

7. Simon strengthened Jerusalem, expanded education, and created coins with ancient Jewish symbols instead of pagan images. How did these actions support both Jewish identity and independence?

8. Josephus says that under Simon, "Every man sat under his own vine and fig tree." What picture of daily life and peace does this image create, and why would it be meaningful after years of war?

9. The author writes that "the seeds of contradiction sprouted quickly" once priests gained political power. What kinds of contradictions might appear when religious leaders also control the state?

10. The chapter claims that "zeal for purity began to taste the power of position." How can sincere religious zeal be changed or corrupted when it becomes closely tied to political authority?

Chapter 7 Herod's Kingdom: The Great Builder
and His Temple

1. How did Pompey's capture of Jerusalem and entry into the Holy of Holies change the political future of Judea?

2. The text says Jewish independence had "flickered; now the lamp dimmed." What does this metaphor suggest about the feelings of the Jewish people under Roman control?

3. In what ways did Antipater's background and role prepare the way for Herod's rise to power?

4. How did Herod's mixed identity as an Idumean in a Jewish world create tension with the people he ruled?

5. The chapter calls Herod's ambition one that "knew no moral restraint." Which actions from the text support this description most clearly?

6. Why might Rome have considered Herod a useful client king, and how did that benefit the empire?

7. What does Emperor Augustus's remark, "Better to be Herod's pig than his son," reveal about Herod's character and reputation?

8. The chapter contrasts Herod's outward adherence to Jewish dietary laws with his violent actions. What does this reveal about the difference between religious appearance and moral behavior?

9. The author says Herod believed "monuments outlive memory." Do you think great building projects can really erase a ruler's cruelty? Why or why not?

10. The chapter hints that God was "weaving history's tapestry toward redemption" during this violent and unstable time. How might this idea challenge the way people usually interpret suffering and political oppression?

Chapter 8 Many Voices, One Hope: The Movements of the Time

1. The chapter says "four great currents of thought flowed—each claiming to represent true Israel." Why might multiple groups all feel they were the most faithful expression of Israel at that time?

2. How did the silence of the prophets and the control of foreign empires shape the spiritual mood of the Jewish people in this period?

3. The author writes that the people believed God had not abandoned them "even if His presence seemed hidden behind Roman banners." What does this image suggest about faith under foreign rule?

4. In what ways can "diversity under pressure" help a faith community grow, rather than simply divide it? Use examples from the chapter to support your answer.

5. The Pharisees began as a response to "corruption" among priests and kings. What problems were they trying to fix, and why did they think ordinary Israelites were the answer?

6. The Pharisees wanted each home to be "a miniature sanctuary." How might this goal change the way families lived their daily lives?

7. Why was the idea of an "oral *Torah*" important for the Pharisees, and how might it affect the way people applied Scripture in everyday situations?

8. How did the Pharisees' belief in resurrection and a final day of judgment influence the way they understood history and personal choices?

9. The chapter describes a "delicate dance" between God's rule over all things and human moral choice. What are some challenges that come from holding both of these ideas at the same time?

10. Because the Pharisees focused on teaching rather than sacrifice, they gained "immense respect among the people." What does this suggest about what

ordinary people most needed from their religious leaders during this time?

Chapter 9

Scrolls by the Dead Sea: Waiting for the End of Days

1. How did the chance discovery of the Dead Sea Scrolls in 1947 change what historians knew about the Bible and Second Temple Judaism?

2. The chapter calls Qumran a "time capsule of Second Temple spirituality." What makes these scrolls more than just old manuscripts?

3. Why did some groups within Israel choose "wilderness over compromise," and what does that decision reveal about their view of faithfulness?

4. The desert is described as both harsh and a place of purification and renewal. How can the same place symbolize suffering and spiritual renewal at the same time?

5. What earlier biblical events in the wilderness (like Sinai, Elijah, or Isaiah's vision) might have inspired the Qumran Community's choice to settle in the desert?

6. The group at Qumran is called the *Yahad*, meaning "the Community." How did their shared lifestyle and strict rules shape their identity and purpose?

7. Why were the Qumran members so disturbed by the corruption and Hellenization of the Jerusalem priesthood that they chose to withdraw completely?

8. The text mentions a "Teacher of Righteousness" and a "Wicked Priest." What does this conflict

suggest about how the community understood true leadership and holiness?

9. The Community Rule describes a two-year probation, shared property, and discipline for even minor sins. What might be the benefits and dangers of living in such a strict religious community?

10. The chapter says they lived with "the rigor of Levites and the anticipation of prophets." How did this combination of careful ritual life and end-times expectation shape their daily choices and emotions?

Chapter 10 Messiah and the Temple: Expectation Fulfilled

1. How does the chapter describe Israel's longing for God to "dwell among His people," and why was the Temple central to that hope?

2. In what ways do the prophets (Isaiah, Micah, Malachi) point to a future "living sanctuary" rather than just another building?

3. How does the picture of Herod's Temple—beautiful, powerful, and permanent—contrast with the social and spiritual unrest in Jerusalem at that time?

4. Why is it significant that ordinary people were praying in the Temple courts while, according to the chapter, the true Presence of God had been born among them without their knowledge?

5. The chapter calls *Yeshua*'s life a "quiet midrash upon the Temple." What do you think this phrase

means, and how might His actions and teachings re-interpret the Temple's purpose?

6. When Simeon holds the infant *Yeshua* and says, "My eyes have seen Your salvation," how does that scene show the Temple's deeper purpose being fulfilled?

7. At age twelve, *Yeshua* says, "I must be in My Father's house." What does this reveal about how He understood His relationship to the Temple and to God?

8. The chapter describes the Temple as a "relational meeting point" rather than a "human stronghold." How does this idea challenge common views of sacred buildings or religious institutions today?

9. Why might John the Immerser's ministry and *Yeshua*'s immersion at the Jordan be an important part of the story of Messiah and the Temple, even though they happen outside Jerusalem?

10. After reading this chapter, how would you explain the claim that in *Yeshua*, "heaven and earth would meet within a single Anointed One"—and how does that reshape the meaning of "Temple"?

Chapter 11 The Last Stand: The Fall of Jerusalem

1. How did Roman taxes and political control create anger and fear among the people of Judea in the first century?

2. Why were pagan symbols near the Temple especially offensive to a nation focused on staying separate from idolatry?

3. The chapter calls Roman rule "Pax Romana," or peace through fear. In what ways was this "peace" actually unstable?

4. How did Passover each year increase both Roman suspicion and Jewish longing for freedom from Rome?

5. What do the actions of governors like Cumanus, Felix, and Florus show about Rome's failure to understand Jewish beliefs and customs?

6. Josephus says, "The whole nation was inflamed, and madness seized the people." What events described in the chapter help explain this reaction?

7. Compare the different responses of the Zealots, Sadducees, Pharisees, and the ordinary people. Which group's response do you find most understandable, and why?

8. How did the plundering of the Temple treasury and the crucifixion of Jews near the city walls push the situation from protest into open revolt?

9. The chapter mentions rumors of angels appearing above the altar promising divine help. How might such stories affect people's willingness to enter a "holy war"?

10. If you had lived in Jerusalem at this time, which pressures (economic, religious, political, or social) would have weighed most heavily on you, and how might that have shaped your choices about revolt or peace?

Chapter 12 Faith Without a Temple: Rebuilding the Spirit

1. Why did the destruction of the Temple in 70 CE make it seem like Israel's world had ended, and how does the Habakkuk quote challenge that feeling of despair?

2. The chapter calls Israel's response "one of history's greatest acts of spiritual resilience." What specific changes show this resilience in action?

3. How did worship shift from Temple sacrifice to study, prayer, and community, and what does that say about the flexibility of faith?

4. Why was Yohanan ben Zakkai's request, "Give me Yavneh and its sages," such a powerful and strategic choice at that moment in history?

5. In what ways did the new academy at Yavneh act as a "new Sanhedrin without altar or king," and how did that help "reweave the fabric of Israel's faith"?

6. The sages at Yavneh asked how to obey *Torah* without a Temple. How do the three pillars—prayer, *Torah* study, and acts of compassion—answer that question?

7. What does Rabban Yochanan's teaching that "the world stands on three things: *Torah*, worship, and deeds of loving-kindness" suggest about where holiness is found?

8. How did replacing animal sacrifices with Tefillah ("the bulls of our lips") change the way an ordinary person could relate to God?

9. Why was standardizing the *Amidah* and facing Jerusalem in prayer an important way to keep a

sense of unity and sacred direction after the Temple's destruction?

10. The chapter mentions both rabbinic Judaism and scattered followers of Messiah learning to serve God among the nations. How might losing the Temple have challenged and also strengthened both groups' faith?

Chapter 13 From Ruins to Renewal: Jewish Faith after 70 CE

1. The chapter describes "three strands of mourning" that formed after the Temple's destruction. In your own words, explain each strand and how it helped Jews remember Jerusalem in daily life.

2. How does turning mourning into a regular practice (like daily prayers for Jerusalem or *Tisha b'Av*) change the way a community experiences grief and hope? Give specific examples from the chapter.

3. The text says that "tears turned into a form of covenant loyalty." What does this phrase mean, and how can sorrow become a sign of faithfulness rather than just pain?

4. Why do you think Jewish tradition chose to mix sorrow into moments of great joy, such as breaking a glass at a wedding or leaving a corner of a house unfinished? What effect might this have on a person's view of life?

5. The chapter asks, "Where could Israel now meet God?" after the Temple was destroyed. Summarize

the rabbinic answer to this question and explain how it reshaped Jewish religious life.

6. The sages at Yavneh reorganized worship around synagogue prayer, *Torah* study, and deeds of loving-kindness. Which of these three pillars do you think would be hardest to keep central in your own life, and why?

7. Isaiah 56:7 calls God's house "a House of Prayer for all nations." How did synagogues take over this role after 70 CE, and what does that suggest about the idea of God's presence no longer being limited to one place?

8. The chapter shows how old Scriptures like Lamentations and the Psalms were reused to interpret new tragedies. Why might re-reading ancient texts during fresh disasters be comforting or powerful for a community?

9. Imagine you are a young Jew living just after 70 CE. How might your experience of God, prayer, and community be different from your grandparents' experience in Temple times? Use details from the chapter to support your answer.

10. In what ways does the post-Temple shift toward words (prayer, study, lament) instead of sacrifices challenge common ideas about where and how people can connect with God today? Give at least one modern application or parallel.

Chapter 14 Early Disciples: The Temple and the Followers of *Yeshua*

1. Why did the early followers of *Yeshua* continue to worship at the Temple even after His resurrection?

2. What were the two main places where early believers gathered, and how were those gatherings different?

3. How did *Yeshua*'s warning about the destruction of Jerusalem affect the early Messianic community?

4. What does the book of Hebrews teach about *Yeshua* as the High Priest, and why was this important after the Temple was destroyed?

5. What does it mean that *Yeshua* is described as the "Temple" in John 2:19–21?

6. How does the idea of *Yeshua* "tabernacling" among us (John 1:14) connect to the Old Testament Tabernacle or Temple?

7. What are some ways the New Testament connects *Yeshua* to Temple roles like Passover Lamb, High Priest, and Mercy Seat?

8. According to the chapter, how do believers become a "spiritual house" or "Temple"? What does that look like in real life?

9. Why is the Holy Spirit (*Ruach HaKodesh*) compared to the Shekhinah presence in the Temple?

10. How did early believers worship "without walls," and what can we learn from their example today?

Chapter 15 A Vision of Restoration: The Future Hope

1. How does the chapter describe God's response to the fall of the first Temple, and what does that suggest about God's character?

2. In what ways does Isaiah's vision of Jerusalem as a city of light give hope to people living in exile or under threat?

3. The chapter says nations will come to Jerusalem "to learn from her." What might it look like for one city to become the teaching center of the world?

4. How do images like swords turned into plowshares and war schools closing help you imagine a world without war?

5. Jeremiah buys a field in a land that is about to be ruined. What does this action communicate about trust in God's promises?

6. What is "new" about the new covenant Jeremiah describes, especially in the idea of God writing *Torah* on people's hearts?

7. The chapter contrasts a house of stone with hearts transformed from within. How is inner change different from just rebuilding walls and gates?

8. The title is "A Vision of Restoration: The Future Hope." After reading this section, how would you define "restoration" in your own words?

9. How might these prophetic visions have encouraged ancient Israel, and how might they speak to people facing crisis or loss today?

10. If you could choose one image from Isaiah or Jeremiah in this chapter to illustrate on a poster, which would you pick and why?

Bibliography

Abegg, Martin, Peter Flint, and Eugene Ulrich, *The Dead Sea Scrolls Bible* (New York: Harper One, 1999).

Arrian, *Anabasis of Alexander*, trans. P. A. Brunt (Cambridge: Harvard University Press, Loeb).

Attridge, Harold W. *The Epistle to the Hebrews* (Philadelphia: Fortress Press, 1989).

Avot de-Rabbi Natan, Version A, chap. 4, in Judah Goldin, trans., *The Fathers According to Rabbi Nathan* (New Haven: Yale University Press, 1955).

Bauckham, Richard. The Bible in the Contemporary World: Hermeneutical Ventures. Grand Rapids: Eerdmans, 2015.

Bourgel, Jonathan. "The Destruction of the Samaritan Temple by John Hyrcanus." Journal of Biblical Literature 135, no. 3 (2016).

Carter, Warren. Matthew and the Margins: A Sociopolitical and Religious Reading. Maryknoll, NY: Orbis Books, 2000.

Cohen, Shaye J. D. From the Maccabees to the *Mishnah*, 3rd ed. (Louisville: Westminster John Knox Press, 2014).

Collins, John J. *The Apocalyptic Imagination* (Grand Rapids: Eerdmans, 2016).

Collins, John J. *The Scepter and the Star* (Grand Rapids: Eerdmans, 2010), 74–90, 120–135; John J. Collins, *The Apocalyptic Imagination* (Grand Rapids: Eerdmans, 2016).

Collins, John J. *The Apocalyptic Imagination: An Introduction to Jewish Apocalyptic Literature*, 3rd ed. (Grand Rapids: Eerdmans, 2016).

Dio, Cassius. *Roman History*, trans. Earnest Cary (Cambridge: Harvard University Press, Loeb).

Dunn, James D. G. *The Partings of the Ways* (London: SCM Press, 2006).

Elbogen, Ismar. *Jewish Liturgy: A Comprehensive History* (Philadelphia: Jewish Publication Society, 1993).

Eusebius, *Ecclesiastical History*, trans. G. A. Williamson (London: Penguin Classics, 1989).

Fine, Steven. *The Arch of Titus: From Jerusalem to Rome—and Back* (Cambridge: Harvard University Press, 2016).

Fox, Robin Lane. *Alexander the Great* (London: Penguin, 2004).

Fruchtenbaum, Arnold G. The Footsteps of the Messiah: A Study of the Sequence of Prophetic Events. 2nd rev. ed. San Antonio, TX: Ariel Ministries.

Grabbe, Lester L. Judaism from Cyrus to Hadrian. Vol. 2, The Roman Period. Minneapolis: Fortress Press, 1992.

Hadas, Moses. "Judaism and the Hellenistic Experience: A Classical Model for Living in Two Cultures." Commentary 42, no. 2 (1966).

Hengel, Martin, *Judaism in the Hellenistic Age* (Philadelphia: Fortress Press, 1974).

Hesiod. Theogony. Translated by Glenn W. Most. Loeb Classical Library 57. Cambridge, MA: Harvard University Press, 2006.

Horsley, Richard A. Bandits, Prophets, and Messiahs: Popular Movements in the Time of Jesus. Harrisburg, PA: Trinity Press International, 1999.

Josephus, Flavius. *Antiquities of the Jews*, trans. H. St. J. Thackeray (Cambridge: Harvard University Press, Loeb).

Josephus, Flavius. *The Jewish War*, trans. G. A. Williamson, rev. E. Mary Smallwood (London: Penguin Classics, 1981).

Koester, Craig R. "Judea during Hellenistic Rule (332 BCE–165 BCE)." Enter the Bible. Luther Seminary, July 19, 2021. Accessed April 4, 2026. https://enterthebible.org/time-period/judea-during-hellenistic-rule/.

Levine, Lee I. "The Age of Hellenism: Alexander the Great and the Rise and Fall of the Hasmonean Kingdom." In Jerusalem: Its Sanctity and Centrality to Judaism, Christianity, and Islam, edited by Lee I. Levine, 134–160. New York: Continuum, 1999.

Macrobius. Saturnalia. 2.4.11.

Magness, Jodi. "Journey to Jerusalem: Pilgrims and Immigrants in the Time of Herod." Biblical Archaeology Review 48, no. 4 (Fall 2022).

Magness, Jodi. The Archaeology of Qumran and the Dead Sea Scrolls. Grand Rapids: Eerdmans, 2002.

Martínez, Florentino García, and Eibert J. C. Tigchelaar, eds. *The Dead Sea Scrolls Study Edition*. 2 vols. Leiden: Brill, 1997–1998.

Mason, Steve trans., *The Jewish War* by Josephus (Peabody, MA: Hendrickson, 2016).

Millar, Fergus. *The Roman Near East* (Cambridge: Harvard University Press, 1993).

Netzer, Ehud. The Architecture of Herod, the Great Builder (Tübingen: Mohr Siebeck, 2006).

Pliny the Younger, *Letters*, trans. Betty Radice (London: Penguin Classics, 1969).

Rappaport, Aharon. "What Motivated Antiochus to Issue His Decrees Against the Jews?" Hakirah: The Flatbush Journal of Jewish Law and Thought 16 (2013).

Richardson, Peter. Herod: King of the Jews and Friend of the Romans (Columbia, SC: University of South Carolina Press, 1996).
Sanders, E. P. Judaism: Practice and Belief, 63 BCE–66 CE. London: SCM Press, 1992.

Suetonius, *The Twelve Caesars*, trans. Robert Graves (London: Penguin Classics, 2007).

The Babylonian *Talmud*: Tractate *Shabbat*. Translated by I. Epstein. London: Soncino Press, 1938. *Shabbat* 21b.

Safrai, Shmuel. *The Jewish People in the First Century, Vol. 2: The Social Structure of the Jewish Community in Palestine in the Period of the Mishnah and Talmud*. Edited by S. Safrai and M. Stern. Assen: Van Gorcum, 1976.

Sanders, E. P. Judaism: Practice and Belief, 63 BCE–66 CE. London: SCM Press.

Satterthwaite, Philip E. "The Temple of Herod." In New Testament History, Culture, and Society: A Background to the Texts of the New Testament, edited by Lincoln H. Blumell, 141–160. Provo, UT: Religious Studies Center, Brigham Young University, 2019.

Schiffman, Lawrence H. *Reclaiming the Dead Sea Scrolls* (Philadelphia: Jewish Publication Society, 1994).

VanderKam, James C. The Dead Sea Scrolls Today. 2nd ed. Grand Rapids: Eerdmans, 2010.

Vermes, Geza. The Complete Dead Sea Scrolls in English. Revised ed. London: Penguin Books, 2011.

Wright, N. T. *The New Testament and the People of God*. Christian Origins and the Question of God, Vol. 1. Minneapolis: Fortress Press, 1992.

Wright, N. T. *Paul and the Faithfulness of God* (Minneapolis: Fortress Press, 2013).

Wright, N. T. *Jesus and the Victory of God* (Minneapolis:
Fortress Press, 1996.

Appendices

Appendix A: Key Dates (586 BCE – 135 CE)

Exile and Persian Restoration

586 BCE – Babylon conquers Jerusalem, destroys Solomon's Temple, and exiles many Judeans.

539 BCE – Cyrus of Persia captures Babylon and permits exiles to return.

538–520 BCE – First waves of return to Judah under Sheshbazzar and Zerubbabel.

516 BCE – Second Temple completed and dedicated in Jerusalem.

458 BCE – Ezra arrives in Jerusalem, strengthening *Torah* observance and teaching.

445 BCE – Nehemiah rebuilds Jerusalem's walls and leads covenant renewal.

Greek Conquest and Hellenistic Pressures

332 BCE – Alexander the Great conquers the Levant; Hellenistic culture spreads.

323 BCE – Alexander dies; his empire divides among generals.

3rd century BCE – Septuagint (Greek *Torah*, then other books) translated in Alexandria.

200 BCE – Judea passes from Ptolemaic to Seleucid control.

Maccabees and Hasmonean Rule

167 BCE – Antiochus IV Epiphanes desecrates the Temple; bans *Torah* and circumcision.

167–164 BCE – Maccabean revolt; Mattathias and Judah Maccabee lead guerrilla resistance.

164 BCE – Temple cleansed and rededicated; origin of Hanukkah.

142–63 BCE – Independent Hasmonean kingdom; priest-kings rule Judea.

Roman Domination and Herod's Temple

63 BCE – Pompey enters Jerusalem; Judea becomes a Roman client state.
37–4 BCE – Herod the Great rules as Rome's client king; massively expands the Temple.
c. 4 BCE–30 CE – Life and ministry of *Yeshua* of Nazareth in Roman Judea.

Revolt, Destruction, and Reorientation

66 CE – Jewish revolt against Rome begins in Galilee and Judea.
70 CE – Titus destroys Jerusalem and the Second Temple; survivors scattered.
73 CE – Fall of Masada, last fortress of the revolt.
c. 70–100 CE – Yavneh period; Pharisaic sages rebuild Judaism around *Torah*, prayer, and study.

Last Jewish Kingdom and Final Roman Measures

132–135 CE – Bar Kokhba revolt; brief Jewish control of Jerusalem before crushing defeat.
135 CE – Hadrian re-founds Jerusalem as Aelia Capitolina, bans Jews from the city, and renames the province Syria Palaestina.

Appendix B: Glossary of People and Terms

Key People
Abraham (*Avraham*) – Patriarch of Israel; recipient of the covenant promises that through his seed all nations would be blessed (Genesis 12:1-3).

Cyrus the Great – Persian king who conquered Babylon and issued the decree allowing Jewish exiles to return and rebuild the Temple (Ezra 1:1-4).

Zerubbabel – Davidic descendant who led early returnees and oversaw rebuilding of the Second Temple's foundations.

Ezra – Priest and scribe who "set his heart to seek the *Torah* of *Adonai*," leading spiritual reform centered on Scripture.

Nehemiah – Persian cupbearer turned governor who rebuilt Jerusalem's walls and organized covenant renewal.

Antiochus IV Epiphanes – Seleucid ruler whose aggressive Hellenization and desecration of the Temple sparked the

Maccabean revolt
Mattathias and Judah Maccabee – Priestly family (Hasmoneans) who led resistance against Antiochus and restored the Temple, origin of the Hanukkah story.

Herod the Great – Roman client king who renovated the Second Temple on a grand scale and ruled Judea with both architectural ambition and brutality.

***Yeshua* of Nazareth** – Jewish teacher and healer proclaimed as Messiah; spoke of His body as the Temple and foretold Jerusalem's destruction.

Rabban Yohanan ben Zakkai – Pharisaic sage who, after 70 CE, helped refocus Jewish life on *Torah*, prayer, and acts of mercy at Yavneh.

Rabbi *Akiva* – Influential second-century teacher, martyred after the Bar Kokhba revolt; central in shaping early rabbinic tradition.

Shimon bar Kokhba – Leader of the 132–135 CE revolt; hailed by some as "son of the star" before Rome's overwhelming response.

Core Terms
Second Temple – The Jerusalem Temple rebuilt after the Babylonian exile (completed 516 BCE), later expanded by Herod, and destroyed by Rome in 70 CE.

Shekhinah – Term in later Jewish tradition for the indwelling presence of God, associated with the Tabernacle, Temple, and later with *Torah* and community.

Torah – "Instruction"; specifically, the Five Books of Moses, and by extension, the broader teaching of God for Israel's life.

Tanakh – Acronym for *Torah* (Instruction), *Nevi'im* (Prophets), and *Ketuvim* (Writings), the Hebrew Bible.
Synagogue (*Beit Knesset*) – "House of gathering"; local assembly for prayer, Scripture reading, and teaching that became central in diaspora life.

Beit Midrash – "House of study"; place where *Torah*, *Mishnah*, and later *Talmud* are studied as a primary form of worship.

Mishnah – Early written compilation of Oral *Torah* (c. 200 CE), organizing *halakhic* traditions that had developed in the Second Temple and Yavneh periods.

Talmud – Rabbinic discussion of *Mishnah* and related traditions (Jerusalem and Babylonian *Talmud*s); foundational to later Jewish law and practice.

Halakhah – "Walking"; the practical legal path derived from *Torah* and rabbinic interpretation, guiding daily Jewish life.

Hellenism – Greek culture and worldview that spread after Alexander, bringing both philosophical opportunity and religious pressure.

Hanukkah – Feast of Dedication, commemorating the Maccabean cleansing and rededication of the Temple after Antiochus' desecration (John 10:22).

Dead Sea Scrolls – Scrolls preserved in caves near Qumran, including biblical manuscripts and sectarian texts, illuminating Second Temple Judaism.

Essenes / Qumran Community – Ascetic Jewish group emphasizing purity, Scripture study, and eschatological expectation; likely linked to the scrolls.

Pharisees – Lay movement stressing *Torah*, Oral Law, and purity in daily life; major stream that shaped post-Temple rabbinic Judaism.

Sadducees – Priestly aristocratic group associated with the Temple establishment, accepting mainly the written *Torah* and rejecting resurrection.

Zealots – Revolutionary factions advocating armed resistance against Rome, prominent during the 66–70 CE revolt.

Messiah (*Mashiach*) – "Anointed one"; in this period, expected Davidic king who would restore Israel, purify the Temple, and bring God's kingdom.

Ekklēsia – Greek for "assembly"; used in the New Covenant writings for communities of *Yeshua*-believers, understood as a living Temple.

Map 1: Judea and the Wider World (Persian to Roman Period)

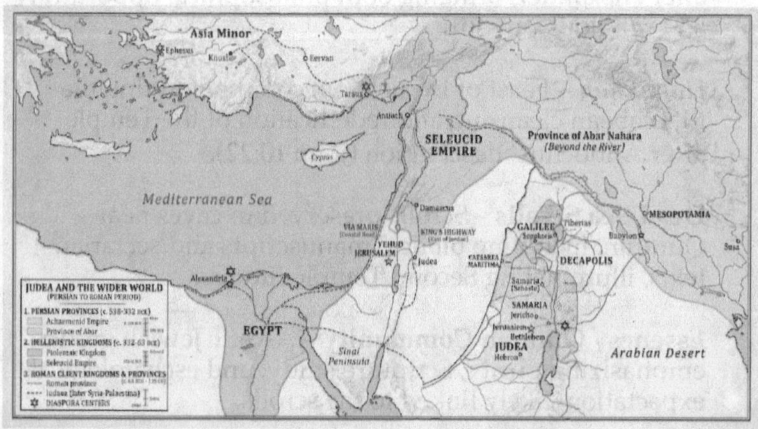

Map 2: Judea in the Time of *Yeshua*

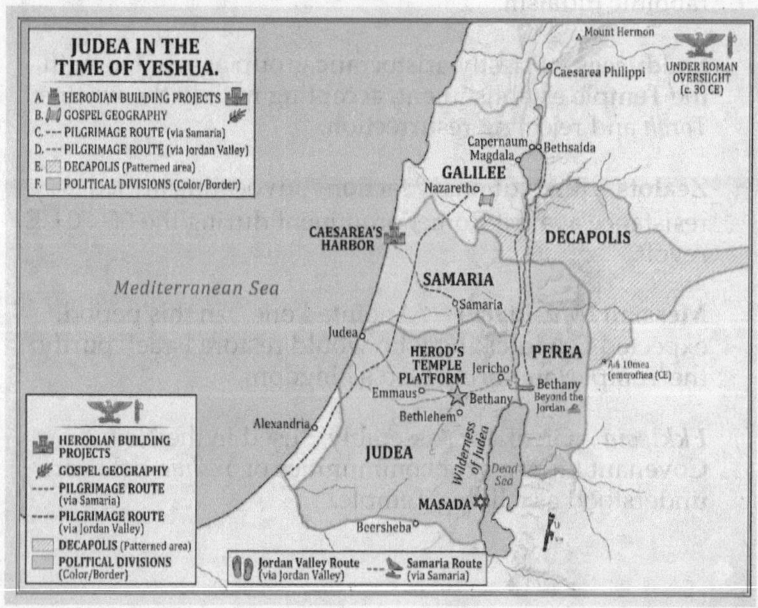

Map 3: Second Temple Jerusalem (Herodian Expansion)

Map 4: Jerusalem After 70 CE

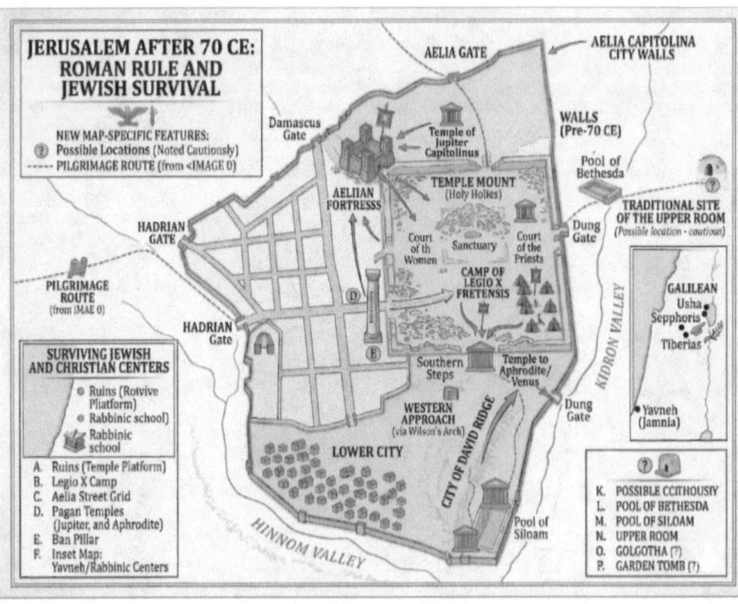